Stella Sandford is Senior Lecturer in Modern European Philosophy at Middlesex University and a member of the *Radical Philosophy* Editorial Collective. She is the author of *The Metaphysics of Love: Gender and Transcendence in Levinas* and a forthcoming book on Plato and sex.

HOW TO READ

Available now

BEAUVOIR

STELLA SANDFORD

W. W. NORTON & COMPANY
New York London

First published in Great Britain by Granta Publications

For information about permission to reproduce selections from this book, write to Permissions, W. W. Norton & Company, Inc., 500 Fifth Avenue, New York, NY 10110

Library of Congress Cataloging-in-Publication Data

Sandford, Stella, 1966–
How to read Beauvoir / Stella Sandford.—1st American ed.
p. cm. — (How to read)
Includes bibliographical references and index.
ISBN-13: 978-0-393-32951-3 (pbk.)
ISBN-10: 0-393-32951-8 (pbk.)
1. Beauvoir, Simone de, 1908–1986. I. Title.
PQ2603.E362Z875 2007
848'.91409—dc22   2006032856

W. W. Norton & Company, Inc.
500 Fifth Avenue, New York, N.Y. 10110
www.wwnorton.com

W. W. Norton & Company Ltd.
Castle House, 75/76 Wells Street, London W1T 3QT

1 2 3 4 5 6 7 8 9 0

CONTENTS

How am I to read *How to Read*?

This series is based on a very simple, but novel idea. Most beginners' guides to great thinkers and writers offer either potted biography or condensed summaries of their major works, or perhaps even both. *How to Read*, by contrast, brings the reader face-to-face with the writing itself in the company of an expert guide. Its starting point is that in order to get close to what a writer is all about, you have to get close to the words they actually use and be shown how to read those words.

Every book in the series is in a way a masterclass in reading. Each author has selected ten or so short extracts from a writer's work and looks at them in detail as a way of revealing their central ideas and thereby opening doors onto a whole world of thought. Sometimes these extracts are arranged chronologically to give a sense of a thinker's development over time, sometimes not. The books are not merely compilations of a thinker's most famous passages, their 'greatest hits', but rather they offer a series of clues or keys that will enable readers to go on and make discoveries of their own. In addition to the texts and readings, each book provides a short biographical chronology and suggestions for further reading, Internet resources, and so on. The books in the *How to Read* series don't claim to tell you all you need to know about Freud, Nietzsche and Darwin, or indeed Shakespeare and the Marquis de Sade, but they do offer the best starting point for further exploration.

Unlike the available second-hand versions of the minds that have shaped our intellectual, cultural, religious, political and scientific landscape, *How to Read* offers a refreshing set of first-hand encounters with those minds. Our hope is that these books will, by turn, instruct, intrigue, embolden, encourage and delight.

Simon Critchley
New School for Social Research, New York

For my beloved London man

ACKNOWLEDGEMENTS

I would like to thank Peter Osborne, Emily Salines and Alison Stone for their comments and suggestions on aspects of this book, and Bella Shand for her editorial work. Thanks to Peter and Ilya for everything else.

INTRODUCTION

In 1948, on her second trip to the USA, Simone de Beauvoir was questioned by an immigration official as to the purpose of her trip. Her visa said 'lectures'. She specified 'lectures on philosophy'. The official asked her to explain: '"What philosophy?" He allowed me five minutes in which to give him a brief account. I said it was impossible.' (*Force of Circumstance*, pp.164–5)

Luckily, it is not my task here to give a brief account of the forty years of Simone de Beauvoir's work, but to explain, through the discussion of exemplary extracts from that work, why she is a thinker we should be reading today. To the extent that this means explaining *how* we should read Beauvoir, the main claim in this book is that she should be read in the light of the philosophical traditions that she inherited and transformed.

Beauvoir is probably best known, internationally, for her role in catalyzing the feminist movements of the second half of the twentieth century with what is undoubtedly her most important work, *The Second Sex*. This is not, in any straightforward way, a traditional philosophical text. Although its theoretical basis is philosophical and it offers an original account of aspects of human existence, as one of the most influential books of the twentieth century its social and political reception was historically far more important than any philosophical understanding of it. But the success of *The Second Sex* has regrettably overshadowed the rest of Beauvoir's work. In particular her early essays, which provide a rubric for a philosophical reading of her later work – including *The Second Sex* – are little known outside a restricted academic circle. The amazing diversity of the rest of Beauvoir's writing is also surprising to those who know little of her beyond *The Second Sex*. The intention of this book, then, is to expose the reader to the full scope of Beauvoir's work, to explain its philosophical basis and originality, and to communicate the sheer pleasure to be had from reading Beauvoir.

One of the most fascinating aspects of Beauvoir's work is her constant development and revision of enduring themes and ideas. Beauvoir's willingness to criticize her own work and the steady formation of her mature philosophical position are in themselves features worthy of note. For this reason, I have chosen to present Beauvoir's work chronologically, highlighting not just the specific arguments in various works but also showing the relationship between them, even where this means that some ideas are later denounced as failures and superseded. To a great extent, the originality and importance of Beauvoir's best work is indebted to the mistakes and false starts that she overcame in order to write them. Beauvoir's major philosophical achievement was the inauguration of the new field of the philosophy of sex and gender. But even where she drew largely on the innovations of others she was an original writer in the application of philosophical ideas to the current issues of the time, many of which are still the current issues of our time. One of Beauvoir's greatest skills was the ability to see and explain the philosophical issues raised by our most ordinary and everyday experiences. Beauvoir saw the world through philosophical eyes, her own and others', and her work teaches us to do the same, encouraging us to disagree with her specific conclusions and to go beyond her.

The first four chapters of this book explain the philosophical basis of Beauvoir's work and show how she sought to provide existentialism with a theory of morality, that is, an account of how existentialist claims about the nature of human existence could form the basis for a guide to ethical action. They show how Beauvoir began to transform existentialist ideas in their application to specific social and political problems, in a variety of genres, as well as explaining the limitations of these works. Chapters 5 to 7 deal with the groundbreaking, socially revolutionary, book *The Second Sex*, making clear the implications of the often-overlooked philosophical ideas informing Beauvoir's social analysis and demonstrating their contemporary relevance. The remaining chapters cover some of Beauvoir's later works, again emphasising the continuing development of Beauvoir's thought and its diversity, culminating in the last major work, *Old Age*.

As is well known, Beauvoir shared her life with another of the twentieth century's most important European philosophers, Jean-Paul Sartre. Theirs was an extraordinary, unconventional and enduring intellectual, emotional and (in the beginning) sexual relationship. Although they never married, did not live together, and had relationships with others, their life-long commitment to each other was more intense than many a bourgeois marriage. However, the linking of their names in the public imagination has not, on the whole, been to Beauvoir's advantage and has often obscured the possibility of a serious understanding of her work. Prurient interest in their relationship has sometimes reduced knowledge of Beauvoir to the level of the tabloids and, on the basis of Sartre's greater and earlier fame, the derogatory characterization of her as 'La Grande Sartreuse' sums up the idea that, intellectually, she is merely derivative of him. It is hoped that this book will help correct this misunderstanding.

For better or worse, Beauvoir and Sartre came to be seen as the living embodiments of the philosophy of existentialism, as both a set of ideas and a way of life. A fantasy of their mid-century Left Bank lives – all black *café* and turtle-necks, *Gitanes* and free love in basement jazz clubs – inspired countless young men and women looking for 'authenticity'. (Armed with this picture, the American publisher Blanche Knopf first mooted the idea of translating *The Second Sex* into English, believing it to be a 'modern-day sex manual' that would sell well amongst young

Americans in thrall to the lure of the life of Saint-Germain-des-Prés.[1]) The cultural force of this fantasy become cliché is evident in the affectionate lampooning of existentialism: the thinly disguised 'emphaticalists' of *Funny Face* (1956), the Left Bank pretensions of Tony Hancock's character in *The Rebel* (1960), and more recently the frequent existentialist skiffs in Biff's *Guardian* cartoons. If these clichés, in the climate of anti-intellectualism that prevails in the Anglophone world, help draw us towards philosophy, so much the better. Away from these caricatures, Beauvoir's and Sartre's books still provide, for many, the first, intoxicating taste of philosophy – a disturbing, exciting opening into the radical questioning of everything that one might have previously taken for granted.

So what is existentialism? The question is complicated by the diversity of the philosophies and other intellectual productions that have attracted the name. In short, however, it may be characterized as that philosophical tradition and orientation concerned with the analysis of 'existence', where 'existence' is the term reserved for the being of the human: its nature, its meaning, its possibilities and its afflictions. This does not mean that existentialism engages in an attempt to isolate a property unique to humanity, the possession of which would qualify one for the ascription 'human'; rather, it undertakes to describe the fundamental characteristics of *existing* as a human in the midst of the world of humans and others. Working from the assumption that human existence is *free* existence – that human action is not in the last instance determined by physical or material factors or by historical or psychological 'fate' – existentialist philosophy has most often been concerned with the implications of freedom in action, in particular the implications for our understanding of morality. Coupled with the conviction that human existence – both as a whole and in relation to each individual – is utterly contingent (that is, not necessitated in any way but simply a fact), we can see how the existentialist preoccupation with freedom and action leads us to the question popularly considered to be the essence of philosophical enquiry: what is the meaning of life?

The fundamental forms of the basic questions of existentialism are easy to mock, but less easy to answer or dismiss. Who am I? Or, in more philosophical terms: what is it to be a human being? What is the *being* of human being (in contrast, say, to the being of an inanimate object, or an idea, or an art work)? Why am I here? Is there a reason or justification for my existence? What is the meaning of my existence? *Is there* a meaning to my existence? And if so, from where does that meaning come? For Beauvoir and Sartre, both convinced atheists, the fact of there being no possible religious answer to these questions gave them their urgency and poignancy. Similarly, all answers that fake the certainty of religion by other means – for example, those purporting to secure the objectivity of morality by attributing the origin of meaning or value to absolute social or historical entities, or to abstract fictions such as 'humanity' – were resolutely disallowed. Their existentialist philosophies shone a harsh and unforgiving spotlight on the freedom and consequent responsibility of human beings, and on our pathetic attempts to avoid or disavow these. Both thinkers were unapologetic if their work was discomforting or worse. Its message was: we're here, there's no external justification or meaning for our existence – get used to it. On the basis of these uncompromising truths the task allocated to us by existentialist philosophy is to assume responsibility for ourselves, for each other and for our world.

Although a European tradition and canon of existentialist works could, retrospectively, be identified as existing by the time of Beauvoir's and Sartre's first 'existentialist' works in the late 1930s and 1940s, the idea that existentialism might be some kind of socially, as well as philosophically, significant movement crystallized around these two French writers. Many factors played a role in this: the technological and social conditions that made possible the figure of the international intellectual; the discrediting of German culture, and in particular of Martin Heidegger's

Nazi-tainted version of existentialism; the 'scandalous' nature of the open relationship between Beauvoir and Sartre and its perceived relation to their philosophies; their increasingly outspoken leftist views and social and political interventions; and, of course, the huge distribution and success of their work. By 1945 they were perceived to be spokespersons for the movement, frequently called upon to explain and justify both it and themselves.

Existentialist philosophy lends itself – for intrinsic reasons – to expression in relatively accessible, non-traditional forms. The fact that Beauvoir and Sartre wrote existentialist novels and occasional essays aided the popularization of their ideas. However, the 'big books' of existentialist philosophy loomed large in the background. Martin Heidegger's *Being and Time* (1927), from which Beauvoir and Sartre took the idea of 'existential analysis', was already philosophically influential in the 1940s but almost unknown outside academia. Sartre's *Being and Nothingness* (1943), his most sustained philosophical work, was in part a reworking of *Being and Time*. Unusually for a work of this kind (a dense, extremely challenging, seven hundred-page, systematic philosophical treatise) *Being and Nothingness* became famous (which is not to say that it was actually widely read). Even now, in undergraduate university courses on existentialism, it is 'the' work of existentialist philosophy.

Due, in part, to the fame and influence of *Being and Nothingness*, and the fact that Beauvoir wrote no equivalent treatise of this kind, scholarly and political controversy surrounds discussion of the relation of Beauvoir's philosophical position to that of Sartre. In her autobiography Beauvoir insisted, on more than one occasion, that Sartre's *Being and Nothingness* had provided her with the philosophical framework within which she worked and that she had nothing to add to it. Beauvoir publicly defended Sartre against detractors (real or perceived) and was at times more Sartrean than Sartre himself, especially in seeming to remain faithful to the basics of *Being and Nothingness* when it was not clear that Sartre himself did. However, at the same time, without ever explicitly criticizing him, Beauvoir produced a body of work that systematically denied certain tenets in *Being and Nothingness* and reorganized its priorities, placing limits on the philosophical conception of freedom that animates Sartre's book and shifting the emphasis on to the lived, embodied aspects of our situation. She contributed elements to the existentialist project that were utterly alien to Sartre's work, fighting with her Sartrean framework as she bent it, more or less successfully, to her intellectual will. From the very beginning, then, even when Beauvoir seemed (and certainly claimed to be) most orthodoxly Sartrean, a uniquely configured Beauvoirian existentialism was emerging.

The reader without prejudice will perhaps be surprised to learn that the question of Beauvoir's status as a philosopher has been the subject of much acrimonious dispute. This concerns not just how good or important a philosopher she is, but, more fundamentally, whether or not she is a philosopher at all. It could not be said that this has reached the level of a debate, since those who would debar Beauvoir from the august title of 'philosopher' do not usually bother to read her work carefully (if at all) or to say why. On the other hand, the committee assembled in her defence is knowledgeable and eloquent. The controversy is political. The need to assert Beauvoir's philosophical credentials is due to two peculiar characteristics of the discipline of philosophy: its historical domination by men and continuing, if archaic, sexism; and its disciplinary narrow-mindedness. Many of its practitioners are unable to recognize philosophical discussion as such unless it conforms to a certain style and terminology and is published in the form of a treatise or in the learned journals that might be displayed in the Senior Common Rooms of certain universities. It helps, in these circumstances, if one is a man. The problem is compounded in the English analytical philosophical tradition by a suspicion, if not hatred, of French intellectuals. Beauvoir scores badly on all points.

The most basic problem with the position against Beauvoir is its inability to see what philosophy *becomes* in Beauvoir's work.

Born in 1908, Beauvoir was one of the first generation of
women in France to be allowed to enter the philosophy *agréga-
tion*, the competitive examination through which an elite is
selected for a professional career in philosophy. She did fantasti-
cally well in what is universally agreed to be one of the toughest
intellectual tests in the European academy. Although Beauvoir
was therefore trained as a philosopher – and ascribed many of her
intellectual virtues to this training – she eschewed the university
career that she could have pursued, in favour of writing. It did
not bother Beauvoir if the more hidebound creatures of academic philosophy decided that she was not 'one of us' – it was
precisely her aim *not* to be. Furthermore, Beauvoir had no
respect for disciplinary boundaries. One of the most distinctive
things about her *oeuvre* is its range across literary forms and intellectual genres. Apart from the philosophical essays, novels, short
stories, plays, autobiography, memoirs, travel journal, magazine
articles, reports, political essays, letters, literary-philosophical
criticism and literary theory, there are the major works that defy
all such classification – *The Second Sex* and *Old Age*. There are
also a number of other works that blend genres: for example, the
mixture of memoir, conversation, interview, homage and criticism that comprises *Adieux: A Farewell to Sartre*. Thus, not only
did Beauvoir move comfortably from one form and discipline to
another, she mixed them together and in some cases pushed at
their limits. The question of the place of philosophy in
Beauvoir's work is not primarily a matter of identifying the traditionally philosophical works or elements within this diversity of
form and discipline. It is a question of the transformation of
philosophy itself, traditionally understood, and the place or role
of philosophical thought in human existence. What does philosophy *become* in its forced confrontation with other disciplines,
with culture and with society? If it is something that the old aca-
demicians cannot recognize, we should be neither surprised nor
troubled, but intrigued.

$$\textbf{1}$$

ANXIETY

Plutarch tells us that one day Pyrrhus was devising projects of conquest. 'We are going to subjugate Greece first,' he was saying. 'And after that?' said Cineas. 'We will vanquish Africa.' – 'After Africa?' – 'We will go on to Asia, we will conquer Asia Minor, Arabia.' – 'And after that?' – 'We will go on as far as India.' – 'After India?' – 'Ah!' said Pyrrhus, 'I will rest.' – 'Why not rest right away?' said Cineas.

Cineas seems wise. What's the use of leaving if it is to return home? What's the use of starting if you must stop? And yet, if I don't first decide to stop, it seems to me to be even more point- less to leave. 'I will not say A,' says the schoolboy stubbornly. 'But why?' 'Because, after that, I will have to say B.' He knows that if he starts, he will never be finished with it: after B, it will be the entire alphabet, syllables, words, books, tests, and a career. Each minute a new task will throw him forward toward a new task, with- out rest. If it is never to be finished, what's the use of starting? Even the architect of the Tower of Babel thought that the sky was a ceiling and that someone would reach it one day. If Pyrrhus could push the limits of his conquests back beyond the earth, beyond the stars and the furthest nebulae, to an infinity that would be constantly fleeing before him, his undertaking would only be more foolish because of it. His efforts would be dispersed without ever coming together for any goal. Viewed by reflection, all human projects therefore seem absurd because they exist only by setting limits for themselves, and one can always overstep these limits, asking oneself derisively, 'Why as far as this? Why not further? What's the use?'

'I found that no goal was worth the trouble of any effort,' said Benjamin Constant's hero. Such are often the thoughts of the adolescent when the voice of reflection awakens in him. As a child, he was like Pyrrhus: he ran, he played without asking himself questions, and the objects that he created seemed to him endowed with an absolute existence. They carried within themselves their reason for being. But he discovered one day that he had the power to surpass his own ends. There are no longer ends; only pointless occupations still exist for him; he rejects them. 'The dice are loaded,' he says. He looks at his elders with scorn: how is it possible for them to believe in their undertakings? They are dupes. Some have killed themselves in order to put an end to this ridiculous illusion. And it was indeed the only way to end it, because as long as I remain alive, Cineas harasses me in vain, saying: 'And after that? What's the use?' In spite of everything, my heart beats, my hand reaches out, new projects are born and push me forward. Wise men have wanted to see the sign of man's incurable folly in this stubbornness. But can a perversion so essential still be called a perversion? Where will we find the truth about man if it is not in him? Reflection cannot stop the élan of our spontaneity.

Pyrrhus and Cineas, pp.90–91.

In her autobiography Beauvoir recounts the goad that led her to write *Pyrrhus and Cineas*, her earliest published philosophical work. 'Madame,' the publisher Jean Grenier asked her, 'are *you* an existentialist?' At this point, in early 1943, Beauvoir associated the philosophy of 'existentialism' with Søren Kierkegaard and Martin Heidegger, and attributed the coining of the word 'existentialist' (the meaning of which she claimed not to understand) to her compatriot Gabriel Marcel. (*The Prime of Life*, pp.547–8) Although we cannot say exactly when Beauvoir first identified herself as an existentialist, in writing *Pyrrhus and Cineas* she was beginning to work out her philosophical position explicitly. She later described the book as an attempt 'to provide existentialist morals with a material content'. (*The Prime of Life*, p.549) For Beauvoir and Sartre, the starting point of existentialism was the individual's consciousness, and all meaning and values ascribed to the world had their source in the individual. Disallowing any appeal to God, or any external moral authority like 'nature', existentialism seemed to many to be a fundamentally amoral, or even immoral, philosophy. Although Beauvoir's existentialist predecessors and peers – Sartre in particular – had claimed that an existentialist morality was possible, no one had actually showed how. Beauvoir's early attempts to flesh out such a moral- ity, explaining exactly how morality could begin with the individual, were her first original contributions to the history of existentialist philosophy. And although Beauvoir's ethics have never been taken up wholesale (as philosophical theories very rarely are) aspects of it (the stress on the individual's relations with others and the social and ideological context of individual action) have made an important contributions to existentialist philoso- phy and are now the subject of renewed interest in Beauvoir's work.

Grenier had proposed that Beauvoir contribute to a volume of essays, 'typical of contemporary ideological trends'. Initially reluctant, Beauvoir nevertheless began writing and three months later was surprised to find that her essay had 'swelled into a small book'. (*The Prime of Life*, p.548) The particular problem that preoccupied her, and which had been the main theme of her recently published novel *The Blood of Others* (1943), was the nature of the relation between the free individual and 'universal reality', or the historically unfolding world of brute facts and other men and women. This was already a central concern in existentialism, to the extent that the nature of the relation was one of the things that it attempted to work out philosophically. But Beauvoir's interpretation of the issue in terms of the individual's anguished struggle against the universal is distinctively original. In the extract above, from the opening paragraphs of *Pyrrhus and Cineas*, Beauvoir sets out some basic existentialist principles in order to present this problem in its most acute form. This way of presenting a problem – drawing it out into its most extreme form – is typical of many of Beauvoir's works. These paragraphs are also typical of Beauvoir's early essays; in particular their openings. A cascade of claims and questions tumble one after another leaving the reader uncertain as to the main point. In the subsequent paragraphs the thematic foci and questions proliferate even further. Very often what Beauvoir specifies as the guiding question at the beginning of her essays is not followed through, or the main thematic focus emerges in such a way as to leave it behind. One might conclude from Beauvoir's work as a whole that editing was not one of her foremost literary skills. In *Pyrrhus and Cineas*, however, as in the other philosophical work of this period, the apparent jumble and waylaying of the argument is a consequence of the breathless vivacity of the writing and a faithfulness to the philosophical principle (attributed originally to Socrates) that one should go where the argument takes one, not lead the argument where one wants it to go. The style reflects the novelty of the content. This is philosophy leaping into an open field. What we now identify as the existentialist assumptions behind the argument were to Beauvoir and her contemporaries relatively new ideas, the consequences of which were only just beginning to be worked through. This is an excited philosophy.

Writing in the first century AD, Plutarch's story is about the adviser Cineas' unsuccessful attempt to moderate king Pyrrhus' militaristic ambition. (After sustaining heavy defeats in a victory against the Romans in 279 BC Pyrrhus famously declared 'one more such victory and I am lost', giving rise to the idea of a 'pyrrhic victory'.) Giving the story an existentialist interpretation, Beauvoir uses the anecdote to reflect on the nature and meaning of human action in relation to the ultimate purpose of human existence. Facing questions of such enormity has made existentialism easy prey for ridicule. However, such ridicule often reveals the nagging insistence of the questions so guilelessly raised here, the little nagging 'what's the use?', the nameless anxiety that quietly accompanies us, especially in our quotidian working and consuming lives.

In Beauvoir's explanation for the uneasiness that accompanies human existence we can see her reliance on certain fundamental existentialist ideas. First, Beauvoir builds on the paradoxical idea that the essence of being human lies in human existence, that is, that the meaning of human existence is not given beforehand (by a God, for example, or by nature) but arises *in existing*. Accordingly, Beauvoir conceives of the human subject as a dynamic movement towards the future. To exist is to project oneself into the future, and this ceaseless movement of projection means that we cannot identify ourselves as a static and enduring essence that simply is what it is. Human existence is a continual process of *becoming*, for each of us a forever unfinished project (death is the cessation, not the completion of life). In this dynamic conception of the human subject, action, broadly conceived, is not what a human being *does*, it is what a human being *is*.

Second, in existentialist philosophy the meaning of human action, which is directed towards the future, is not determined by any external authority or set of circumstances, but is internal to that action itself, in the relation of an action to its end, its 'telos' or goal. For example, the meaning of any one of Pyrrhus' conquests is, for him, not determined by world history or by the gods, but by the goal of the conquest itself. Similarly, the meaning of human existence is itself not externally imposed or given, but internal to the understanding of the action – the 'projects' – that constitute it. And herein lies the problem.

In the extract above, Beauvoir writes that all human action is conceived and undertaken in relation to a specific end, and only makes sense in relation to that end. Any action at all could suffice to illustrate this, but let us use Beauvoir herself as an example. In 1943 Beauvoir conceived the project of writing a philosophical essay, thinking to herself, as she wrote in her autobiography, that she 'has something to say about . . . the relationship of individual experience to universal reality'. (*The Prime of Life*, p.548) This project was necessarily limited by the projected goal: the production of the essay (rather than, say, a philosophical system spanning twenty volumes, or a comic opera concerned with the same theme). Without this projected end – or at least some projected end – all efforts to communicate something on her chosen topic would, as she wrote, 'be dispersed without ever coming together for any goal'. And yet as soon as she embarks on the essay, the projected end is revealed to be no more than an arbitrary limit. Why stop with an essay? Why not a twenty-volume work? If the overstepping of this arbitrary limit is easily conceived, what hold can the projection of the original goal have over me? On reflection, Beauvoir says, we see that all human action, though it is made meaningful in relation to its projected ends, is at the same time rendered otiose by them. Either we must set ourselves no limits, in which case we act haphazardly, or we restrict ourselves with goals that are immediately outdated. And if the limits we necessarily set for ourselves as the living goals of our actions immediately become no more than a deadening limitation, is not all human action, and thus human existence, thereby absurd?

This is not to conclude that all human action and existence is indeed absurd, it is merely to raise the *possibility* that it might be, based on the assumption that it is in the nature of human action to continually surpass itself. In typical existentialist fashion, Beauvoir is demanding that we look the unpleasant or threatening possibility of the absurdity of human existence squarely in the face, rather than comforting ourselves with convenient lies or conventional answers. In fact, it is precisely the confrontation with and rejection of the convenient lies or conventional answers that is at issue. Beauvoir describes this confrontation as a stage in the awakening philosophical consciousness of each individual. The 'voice of reflection awakens' during the *adolescence* of the philosophical subject. The agonies of teenage angst are no doubt comical to mature reflection, but it is to Beauvoir's great credit that she is able to give them a philosophical dignity. The child, she says elsewhere, lives in a world in which it takes no responsibility for the meanings and values that it is taught to ascribe to things, what Beauvoir calls a 'serious' world. (*The Ethics of Ambiguity*, p.35) The totality of objects and relations that make up the world seem, to the child, to be 'endowed with an absolute existence' – they seem to need no justification or explanation for their existence, which is unquestioningly taken for granted. More importantly, Beauvoir implies, the child takes its own existence for granted. The 'crisis of adolescence' (*The Ethics of Ambiguity*, p.39) is the end of this security and the beginning of our famed 'existential angst', when we 'assume' our subjectivity and are forced to begin to take responsibility for our own existence and the meanings it may have for us. The expressions of adolescent reflection on this crisis may take stereotypical forms, but, as Beauvoir shows, they may be translated into a vocabulary that reveals their philosophical truth. When the adolescent says petulantly that she 'did not ask to be born' she realises that her existence is sheer contingency, that there is no 'reason' for having been born. If the adolescent 'looks at his elders with scorn' it is because the nihilism of this crisis seems to him to be the only authentic response to the perceived pointlessness of existence. 'Some have killed themselves', Beauvoir says. It is worth taking that point seriously, instead of ridiculing and despising the young.

Although the adolescent features literally in Beauvoir's thought, the idea of the adolescence of the philosophical subject has a broader significance. The claims about the 'child' and the 'adolescent' in this extract are not merely empirical claims about stages of physiological and psychological maturation, but also

existential claims about the human subject. (If they were merely
empirical claims we would have to disagree with some of them.
Where is the child that does not ask questions about its existence?) In *Pyrrhus and Cineas*, as in other of Beauvoir's works of
this period, she follows a philosophical model provided by G. W. F.
Hegel's remarkable, and famously difficult, *Phenomenology of Spirit*
(1807). In this book Hegel writes what he calls a 'science of the
experience of consciousness', an account of the historical development of mind or spirit (*Geist*), ascending in stages from the
simplest and retrospectively inadequate form of knowledge to
'absolute knowledge' or knowledge of the truth. Very often
these stages are represented by distinct figures, frequently associated with a particular philosophical position – for example, the
'unhappy consciousness' of the religious man alienated from
the Absolute, or the 'beautiful soul' of the moral idealist,
untainted by any real moral relation to the world. The movement from one stage to another is described as a 'journey' of the
experience of consciousness, and this must be understood at
several levels simultaneously. Each consciousness – each one of
us – undertakes this journey for ourselves. At the same time,
each one of us lives at a particular point in the development
of world history and thus at a particular point in the journey of
universal spirit.

In the extract from *Pyrrhus and Cineas* the 'child' and the
'adolescent' are like the figures in Hegel's *Phenomenology of Spirit*,
representing stages on the journey of the development of consciousness in this multi-layered sense. Adolescence is a stage of
individual maturation, but it is also a stage of individual philosophical development that is not age-specific, and a stage of the
historical development of philosophy. Thus these opening paragraphs from *Pyrrhus and Cineas* refer not only to the philosophical
awakening of each individual (Beauvoir included), but also to the
philosophical awakening of Beauvoir's generation of philosophers – an awakening to the hard truths of existentialism – and
even to the adolescence of the history of philosophy itself. This

last point seems odd, given that philosophy in the 1940s was in a sense already 'old'; at least 2,000 years old, according to the usual European histories. But philosophy, for Beauvoir, was adolescent in only just beginning to rid itself of the taken-for-granted certainties of its admittedly extended childhood. Specifically, philosophy was only just beginning to rid itself of the yoke of religious – for Beauvoir, Christian – certainty, of the comforting religious justification for human existence and the convenient religious explanations that gave it meaning and value.

In the Introduction to his *Phenomenology of Spirit* Hegel describes the 'road' on which consciousness travels as 'the pathway of *doubt*, or more precisely . . . the way of despair'. At each stage in the education of consciousness, the realization of the inadequacy of its previous assumptions is experienced as 'a state of despair about all the so-called natural ideas, thoughts, opinions, regardless of whether they are called one's own or someone else's'. [2] In the experience of despair we fail to see, according to Hegel, that our rejection of our previous beliefs is already a positive step, that our negation is 'determinate', meaning that its result is more than just nothing; it leads to something else. In *Pyrrhus and Cineas*, by raising the possibility that all human action and existence is absurd, Beauvoir dramatises just such an experience of despair in the opening paragraphs. Adolescence is the experience of despair without the insight into the positive result of its negation of previous beliefs. If we read no further in *Pyrrhus and Cineas* we would be left at this stage of despair, but of course the book does not end here.

Beauvoir goes on to argue that it is in the impact of my actions on others that the possibility of the justification for my action arises. The paradox of action, according to Beauvoir, is that although the goal of every action is what gives it meaning as an action, that end is immediately capable of being surpassed, potentially rendering the action meaningless. To fend off this meaninglessness we seek for our action a goal that cannot be surpassed. If we imagine that this means we should aim at an

infinite end we are doomed to failure as 'our efforts would be
dispersed without ever coming together for any goal'. An infinite
goal is a meaningless goal for a finite being. According to
Beauvoir, however, the one reality that I cannot transcend or surpass is the reality of the freedom of another human being. If,
Beauvoir argued, the ends of my actions are taken up by other
people and made the ends of their actions too, the end of my
action has taken on a form in which it cannot be surpassed by
me. In the simplest terms this means that my own projects can be
justified in their becoming the projects of my fellow human
beings. I need my fellow human beings, 'these foreign freedoms', Beauvoir writes, 'because once I have surpassed my own
goals, my actions will fall back upon themselves, inert and useless, if they have not been carried off [by others] toward a new
future by new projects'. (*Pyrrhus and Cineas*, p.135) In so doing
the others recognize the validity of my actions and ends and
thus justify them, rescuing them from their potential absurdity.
For Beauvoir this necessity provides us with the rational basis of
morality. Others are only able to make my projects their own if
they have the 'health, leisure, security, and the [social and polit-
ical] freedom to do with themselves what they want . . . I must
therefore strive to create for men situations such that they can
accompany and surpass my transcendence.' (*Pyrrhus and Cineas*,
p.137)

Some twenty years later, in the second volume of her autobiography, Beauvoir was under no illusions about the success or
strength of this solution. It fails, she says there, in assuming that
the individual hammers out their project on their own and only
then asks her fellow human beings to endorse it, instead of recognizing the role that others play in all my concerns from the
very beginning. Beauvoir proceeds as if we work out our projects solitarily, and then go looking for others to take them up,
but the truth is that the others are always already there, as no
human being lives or acts in isolation. The mistaken 'subjec-
tivism' of *Pyrrhus and Cineas* is, Beauvoir says, coupled with a

streak of idealism – a tendency to seek solutions to problems in the realm of ideas, rather than in human relations in the world itself – 'that deprived my speculations of all, or nearly all, their significance'. (*The Prime of Life*, pp.549–50) She might also have added that the morality of *Pyrrhus and Cineas* is wholly self-serving. 'I ask for health, knowledge, well-being, and leisure for men' (*Pyrrhus and Cineas*, p.137) only because *I need* their freedom to justify my actions, not because their health and so on is something worth striving for in its own right. Thus Beauvoir was right to see, on reflection, that the ad hoc and unconvincing solution to the problems raised at the beginning of *Pyrrhus and Cineas* was not where the interest of the book lies. 'This first essay only interests me today,' she wrote in the early 1960s, 'insofar as it marks a stage in my development.' (*The Prime of Life*, p.550) In the same vein we might – quite without contempt – see *Pyrrhus and Cineas* as an expression of Beauvoir's philosophical late-adolescence, where what is of most importance is the critical questioning of received opinion and the rejection of old certainties. To this extent, these extracts demonstrate Beauvoir's willingness to step into the unknown and her ability to give philosophical voice to the kinds of 'adolescent' anxieties and thoughts that mark the dawning of philosophical reflection. Moreover, these anxieties persist in *Pyrrhus and Cineas*, repressed but not overcome by the alleged solution to the existential problems. In particular, they return explicitly in Beauvoir's final reflections and conclusions, where she acknowledges that my projects cannot be justified by being taken over by another precisely because they are then no longer *my* projects. The real conclusion at the end of *Pyrrhus and Cineas* is that we act – we *must* act – despite and in the face of the paradoxes of action: 'We must assume our actions in uncertainty and risk, and that is precisely the essence of freedom.' (*Pyrrhus and Cineas*, p.139) The answer to the problem is that there is no answer. This is the deepest truth of our permanent adolescence. The challenge is to see in it something more than mere negation.

This is what we now think of as classic existentialism. It renders comprehensible, if not justifiable, the popular view of existentialism as a gloomy and pessimistic philosophy for adolescents. But in the last lines of these extracts from *Pyrrhus and Cineas* Beauvoir has a surprise for us up her sleeve. 'In spite of everything,' she writes, 'my heart beats, my hand reaches out, new projects are born and push me forward.' I am not a thing, she continues a few pages later, but 'a project of self toward the other . . . a spontaneity that desires, that loves, that wants, that acts'. (*Pyrrhus and Cineas*, p.93) These lines suggest that the necessity for us to act in the full acknowledgement of the paradoxes of action and the potential meaninglessness of existence is not done grudgingly or in resignation but, on the contrary, in joy. Nothing suppresses 'the 'élan of our spontaneity', the upsurge of life itself, or vitality. Fresh desires, the impulse to love – just 'wanting' in general – continue to assert themselves despite the 'pessimistic' conclusions of philosophical reflection and this, in the end, is the true paradox of action.

2

AMBIGUITY

'The continuous work of our life,' says Montaigne, 'is to build death.' . . . Man knows and thinks this tragic ambivalence which the animal and the plant merely undergo. A new paradox is thereby introduced into his destiny. 'Rational animal', 'thinking reed', he escapes from his natural condition without, however, freeing himself from it. He is still a part of this world of which he is a consciousness. He asserts himself as a pure internality against which no external power can take hold, and he also experiences himself as a thing crushed by the dark weight of other things. At every moment he can grasp the non-temporal truth of his existence. But between the past which no longer is and the future which is not yet, this moment when he exists is nothing. This privilege, which he alone possesses, of being a sovereign and unique subject amidst a universe of objects, is what he shares with all his fellow-men. In turn an object for others, he is nothing more than an individual in the collectivity on which he depends.

As long as there have been men and they have lived, they have felt this tragic ambiguity of their condition, but as long as there have been philosophers and they have thought, most of them have tried to mask it.

. . . At the present time there still exist many doctrines which choose to leave in the shadow certain troubling aspects of a too

complex situation. But their attempt to lie to us is in vain.
Cowardice doesn't pay. Those reasonable metaphysics, those consoling ethics with which they would like to entice us only
accentuate the disorder from which we suffer. Men of today seem
to feel more acutely than ever the paradox of their condition.
They know themselves to be the supreme end to which all action
should be subordinated, but the exigencies of action force them
to treat one another as instruments or obstacles, as means. The
more widespread their mastery of the world, the more they find
themselves crushed by uncontrollable forces.

    . . . In spite of many stubborn lies, at every moment, at every
opportunity, the truth comes to light, the truth of life and death,
of my solitude and my bond with the world, of my freedom and
my servitude, of the insignificance and the sovereign importance
of each man and all men . . . Since we do not succeed in fleeing
it, let us therefore try to look the truth in the face. Let us try to
assume our fundamental ambiguity. It is in the knowledge of the
genuine conditions of our life that we must draw our strength to
live and our reason for acting.

                                     The Ethics of Ambiguity, pp.7–9.

In *Pyrrhus and Cineas* Beauvoir described the paradox of action
both negatively and positively. Negatively, it is evident in our
constant tendency to move beyond (to 'surpass') the goals we set
ourselves, rendering those goals potentially meaningless.
Positively, it is evident in the irrepressible 'upsurge' of joyous
vitality that presses us ever forward to new goals despite the
potential meaninglessness that our reflections reveal. Beauvoir
does not deal explicitly with the relation between these two
points of view in *Pyrrhus and Cineas*, and we seem to be left with
an unresolved contradiction in her thought. However, by the
time of *The Ethics of Ambiguity*, a few years later, Beauvoir had
raised this contradiction to a philosophical principle, that of the
'fundamental ambiguity' of human existence itself. The contradiction is no longer a fault or oversight, it is a fundamental

feature of human existence, the experience of which may be described and explained in philosophical terms.

The extract above, taken from the opening pages of *The Ethics of Ambiguity*, sets out the nature and consequences of this fundamental ambiguity in the starkest terms. Again, it is typical of Beauvoir's early essays. Beauvoir begins at full speed, presenting a series of contradictions out of which emerge some bold claims and ambitious proposals. The difficulty faced in understanding these paragraphs is due, in part, to this headlong rush into the central point of the book before that point has been explained. We begin, as epic forms of poetry often begin, *in media res* – in the middle of things – but without quite understanding where it is that we are. These passages demonstrate something of Beauvoir's pedagogic strategy and literary style. She almost always throws the hard stuff at us first, and never leaves her climaxes to the end. She flatters the reader with her presumption of their intelligence, in return for which she demands that the reader puts in some work.

One of the most arresting things about this extract is its hyperbole. The fundamental characteristic of human existence, its ambiguity, is twice described as 'tragic'. The human condition is 'the disorder from which we suffer'. We are 'crushed by the dark weight of things', 'by uncontrollable forces' and, perhaps unsurprisingly, the troubling truth of our existence is assumed to be something that we fear to look in the face. This dramatic excess is no doubt partly rhetorical. But it is not incidental to the substance of the extract and indeed gives us the clue to its interpretation.

Published in 1947, *The Ethics of Ambiguity* is one of the symptoms of the post-war intellectual anxiety of Beauvoir and her contemporaries. In large part, the abiding interest of Beauvoir's work of this period concerns the ways in which it mirrors, philosophically, the social and political turmoil of its time. In her autobiography Beauvoir vividly describes the often surreal 'normality' of life in Paris under German occupation, as well as its more dramatic aspects: the death of friends, the fear of more death, the bombs, the dangers, the thrill and fear in resistance, the nauseating compromises of collaboration or even of survival. After the liberation, the sickening and almost unbelievable news of the Nazi death camps meant that the period of reflection inaugurated by the war intensified rather than abated. Questions that can seem abstract to the contemporary reader were, for Beauvoir and her friends, concrete and pressing questions about their everyday lives. What does it mean to act in the context of the occupation and the resistance? What constitutes an act of resistance? What constitutes an act at all in the context of collaboration? Is inaction a form of action? How can we decide to act when we cannot know the possible consequences of our actions? Is an act of resistance that results in the death of one's comrades a justifiable act? In these circumstances, as Beauvoir reflected painfully and as honestly as possible on her situation, the vocabulary of tragedy and its crushing weight does not seem so extraordinary or comic. In this respect, *The Ethics of Ambiguity* is a philosophical rendition of some of the most acute social and political dilemmas of its time.

Given this context it is no longer the hyperbole of these passages that seems remarkable, but the nature of the philosophical account. The urgent and often quite specific dilemmas of the war period and its aftermath are transformed into general – and to some extent trans-historical – claims about the tragic nature of human existence itself. In the first paragraph at least four separate and highly condensed points coalesce to deliver the opening blow. Each implicitly identifies a pair of apparently opposed terms and the postulation of a paradoxical relation between the terms in each pair, insofar as they refer to human existence.

First, death is not the opposite of life, but its constant companion. This does not mean that the living must expect to be bereaved, but that death is internal to each living life. Life begins with the seed of death already growing within it. Although this is true of all organisms, the tragedy of human existence is that we are aware of it. This leads to the second point. We are not con-demned to live according to blind nature, acting only on instinct, as some interpretations of the 'scientific' approach to human life maintain. A conscious awareness of self, an ability to reflect on nature, distinguishes human from animal or plant life and human culture liberates us from a merely natural existence. And yet we do not free ourselves from our natural condition. We die and decompose like all organic matter. Further, our experience of ourselves as pure 'internality', the untouchable inner privacy of consciousness, does not prevent us being crushed by the weight of the external world. Able to assert ourselves as more than simply one thing among many in the world, we are nonetheless constantly revealed to be thing-like. Beauvoir turns this point over and looks at it from several different angles. Although I am for myself in the position of absolute subject, in the eyes of others I am easily reduced to an object. What, from my point of view makes me unique – the fact of my being a singular subjec-tivity – is, from another point of view, what makes me the same as everyone else. I assert myself as an individual, and yet my 'individuality' is only comprehensible in so far as I am part of a collectivity in which my individuality recedes.

The most difficult point nestles somewhat awkwardly among the others. At every moment, Beauvoir writes, we can 'grasp the non-temporal [*intemporelle*] truth' of our existence. That is, at every moment we can see what is eternally true of human exis-tence rather than what happens to be true at this or that particular time. This is confusing because the idea of eternity seems to conflict with Beauvoir's commitment to think through the consequences of human finitude. But here she means only to say that at every moment we can grasp something of the ambigu-ous truth of human existence insofar as that truth is not dependent on the contingencies of material, temporal existence. At the same time, however, each of these 'moments' in which we grasp this truth is, strictly speaking, nothing. Each present moment is nothing without its relation to the past and the future, and thus the 'non-temporal' truth of our existence is always sub-ordinated to the facts of its temporal span.

All these points lead to the same conclusion. Each time we try to identify human existence with one of the terms in various oppositions (culture as opposed to nature; internal consciousness as opposed to external objectivity; individuality as opposed to universality; timeless truth as opposed to contingent fact) we find it also immediately identified with the other term too. The either-or logic of rational thought (the logic of non-contradiction) cannot do justice to the messy ambiguity of human existence, where the both-and logic of contradiction holds sway. Human existence is both natural and not-natural; the human subject is both a unique internality and a common external object; we both stand out from and are ultimately absorbed in the mass of humanity.

These paradoxes, expressed in a variety of different ways, are central to most existentialist philosophy. Beauvoir's specific contribution was to identify them as aspects of the most fundamental characteristic of human existence: its *ontological ambiguity*.[3] Although she was not the first to propose a philosophical concept of ambiguity (it was, for example, a feature of Maurice Merleau-Ponty's *Phenomenology of Perception*, which Beauvoir reviewed on its publication in 1945), she was the first to develop it at any length. In characterising the experience of ambiguity as an existential problem – a site of tension for the individual – and in then attempting to make this the basis for morality, Beauvoir was moving boldly into a field in which no one had previously ventured. The 'ambiguity' of human existence does not just refer to the fact that we can understand human existence in multiple and perhaps contradictory ways. The ambiguity is not semantic. It means that human being is, *in its very being*, ambiguous. To be human is to *be* a creature of contradictions, to *exist* (and not just to be understood) in different and contradictory ways simultaneously.

The most important formulation of this ambiguity – which is presumed but not made explicit in these passages – is that human existence is ontologically ambiguous, comprised of both freedom and 'facticity'. The freedom in question here is not physical (freedom from chains), political (freedom from oppression) or social (freedom from convention). It is ontological: freedom to act, to choose to do this rather than that when we could have done otherwise, a freedom that makes us responsible for our actions. According to Beauvoir we *are* freedom in this sense. Human being *is* free being. At the same time, the brute fact of each human existence confronts it as something altogether beyond our choice: this is what, following Martin Heidegger, she calls our 'facticity'. Being also a part of the world like any other thing, the putting into effect of our freedom immediately congeals into the solidity of our facticity. And although I may be, for myself, a free conscious being forever surging forward to the future with continually renewed projects, certain experiences reveal to me that for others I am often no more than the exterior form that our brute existence assumes. For ourselves we are conscious subjectivity; for others we are 'an instrument or obstacle', one more object in amongst so many others.

Beauvoir claims that we have all felt or suffered this 'tragic ambiguity'. But what, precisely, is 'tragic' about it? For Beauvoir it is the fact that these two aspects of existence never coincide. As free conscious subjectivity, we are the absolute origin of the meaning of and justification for our actions, but we are *not* responsible for our own facticity. In the simplest terms, we did not choose to exist, and nothing necessitated our existence. Although the justification for every decision and act lies with us, there is no meaning of or justification for the very fact of our existence. Why do I exist? There is no reason for my existence. Unable to redeem the sheer contingency of the brute fact of our existence, the meaning of everything else we do – the meaning that we ourselves give it – threatens to collapse into meaninglessness or absurdity.

Beauvoir herself admits that it is not hard to see how existentialism gained itself the reputation of 'a philosophy of the absurd and of despair'. (*Ethics of Ambiguity*, p.10) This was the common response of the Christian Right, objecting to the absence of God, of the Communist Left, objecting to the absence of the idea of a common historical task, and of the lay reader, over-whelmed by the critical and confrontational nature of the philosophy. And it is true, Beauvoir says, that this account of human existence, taken by itself, does not offer any hope against the ultimate absurdity of existence in the sense that it offers no way out of its pessimistic conclusion. Perhaps, then, the tragedy of our ambiguous existence is precisely the inevitable failure of any attempt to overcome the ambiguity and escape the threat of meaninglessness. Or perhaps the tragedy – thus far at least – is that, despite this, we keep on trying.

However, just as the gloomy conclusions of *Pyrrhus and Cineas* are challenged there by Beauvoir's claims about the unquench-able upsurge of vitality, the irrepressibility of desire, so here the hopelessness of the fundamental ambiguity of existence in *The Ethics of Ambiguity* is undercut with a surprising claim. The inevitable failure of our efforts to overcome ambiguity is itself, Beauvoir writes, ambiguous. This failure can be made into the positive basis for morality. It is precisely our failure to justify our existence from within ourselves that leads us to appeal to the existence of others. Only in the clear-sighted acceptance of the truth of the ambiguity of existence, with all its 'troubling aspects', do we see how we are bound to other human beings in our need for them to justify our existence for us: 'Only the free-dom of others keeps each one of us from hardening in the absurdity of facticity.' (*Ethics of Ambiguity*, p.71) Beauvoir exhorts us to 'assume', to take on, our fundamental ambiguity, rather than deny it, and describes the process of this acceptance as 'a matter of a conversion'. (*Ethics of Ambiguity*, p.13) *The Ethics of Ambiguity* is thus an evangelical text, and despite the apparent pessimism of its tragic account of human existence, in attempt-ing to found a morality on this very basis it represents the triumph of optimism.

It is hard, however, to escape the conclusion that Beauvoir's optimistic coup de grâce – impressive though it is from one point of view – is but the latest of those 'consoling ethics' with which philosophers like to 'entice us'. In her own harsh judgement a decade and a half later, Beauvoir deplored the hollow nature of her solution in *The Ethics of Ambiguity*, putting its failure down to the idealism that blemished much of her work of this period. Its 'idealism' consists in the fact that it offers no more than an abstract, generalized account of how to think about morality, without being able to show how this might be relevant to any particular case. Further, it presumes that moral decision and action is the outcome of rational reflection on universal themes, rather than a compromise based on the specific, concrete circumstances of each unique situation. 'I was in error,' she later said, 'when I thought I could define a morality independent of a social context.' (*Force of Circumstance*, p.76) That is, Beauvoir failed to see that the apparently universal dilemmas outlined in this extract were in fact the specific problems of the intellectual bourgeois elite to which she belonged. In the context of the post-war settlement, of colonialism and the often violent processes of decolonization and the coming cold war, to search for a morality to which each individual could rationally commit was to overlook the necessity for a political response which would not be about the individual's negotiation of their ambiguity. If *The Ethics of Ambiguity* is best read as an attempt to render the social and political turmoil of the times in philosophical terms, it also reveals the inadequacy of Beauvoir's political response, as she herself was later only too willing to accept, criticizing the individualism of this early work. To the extent that the realization of this failure sparked an intellectual-political crisis for Beauvoir, it signals the beginning of a turning point in her work, and the outcome is by no means merely negative. The 'failure' of *The Ethics of Ambiguity* is thus, of course, fittingly ambiguous.

3

VENGEANCE

Under the Nazi oppression, faced with traitors who have made us their accomplices, we saw poisonous sentiments bloom within our hearts of which we never before had any presentiment. Before the war we lived without wishing any of our fellow humans any harm. Words like vengeance and expiation had no meaning for us. We scorned our political or ideological opponents rather than detesting them. And as for individuals like assassins and thieves, whom society denounced as dangerous, they did not seem to be our enemies. To our eyes their crimes were only accidents provoked by a regime that did not give everyone an equal chance. These people did not compromise any of the values that we were attached to [. . .] Conscious of our privilege, we forbade ourselves to judge them. And we would not have wanted to align ourselves with tribunals that persisted in defending an order we disapproved of.

Since June 1940 we have learned to rage and hate. We have wished humiliation and death on our enemies. And today each time a tribunal condemns a war criminal, an informer, a collaborator, we feel responsible for the verdict. Since we have desired this victory, since we have craved these sanctions, it is in our name that they judge, that they punish. Ours is the public opinion that expresses itself through newspapers, posters, meetings, the public opinion that these specialized instruments are designed to satisfy. We were pleased at the death of Mussolini, at the hanging of the Nazi executioners at Kharkov, with the tears of Darnand. In so doing we have participated in their condemnation. Their crimes have struck at our own hearts. It is our values, our reasons to live that are affirmed by their punishment . . .

It is not a small thing to suddenly find oneself a judge, much more an executioner. During the years of the occupation we claimed this role with enthusiasm. Then, hate was easy. When we read the articles of *Je suis partout*, when we heard on the radio the voice of Ferdonnet or Hérold Paquis, when we thought about the arsonists or Oradour, of the torturers of Buchenwald, of the Nazi leaders and their accomplices, the German people, we said to ourselves in an outburst of anger, 'They will pay.' And our anger seemed to promise a joy so heavy that we could scarcely believe ourselves able to bear it. They have paid. They are going to pay. They pay each day. And the joy has not risen up in our hearts.

No doubt our disappointment is due in part to circumstances. The purge has not been straightforward. Many of the worst war criminals met such a brutally disastrous end that it did not have the appearance of an atonement; others remain out of reach. The attitude of the German people stymies our hate. But this is not enough to explain why a revenge so eagerly desired has left this taste of ashes in our mouths. It is the idea of punishment itself that is at issue here. Now that we feel in their true concreteness the sentiments and attitudes designated by the words 'vengeance', 'justice', 'pardon', 'charity', they have assumed a new meaning that surprises and worries us. Legal sanctions no longer appear to us to be simple police measures that still retain a reflection of past blind beliefs. All of us have more or less felt it: the need to punish, to avenge ourselves. We would like to better understand what this need represents for someone today. Is it well founded? Can it be satisfied?

'An Eye for an Eye', pp.245–47.

In her autobiography Beauvoir wrote that in early 1945 she and
Sartre were still irritated by the label 'existentialist' that was auto-
matically applied to their work. But by the autumn of that year
they had given up protesting against it and decided instead to
embrace it, using it for their own purposes. Without having
planned it, she wrote, 'what we launched early that fall turned
out to be an "Existentialist Offensive". . . . We were astonished by
the furore we caused.'(*Force of Circumstance*, p.46) Sartre published the first two volumes of his trilogy *The Roads to Freedom*
(*The Age of Reason* and *The Reprieve*) and delivered his famous
lecture on existentialism and humanism, now probably the best-
known (although not the best) text on European existentialism.[4]
Beauvoir's second novel, *The Blood of Others*, appeared just before
the opening of her first play, *Useless Mouths*, and she delivered her
now famous lecture on the relationship between philosophy and
the novel, 'Literature and Metaphysics'. At the same time, the
first issues of the review that Beauvoir and Sartre had been plan-
ning for some time – *Les temps modernes* – came rolling off the
presses. Henceforth, Beauvoir recalled, 'a week never passed
without the newspapers discussing us' (*Force of Circumstance*, p.
46), both their ideas and their lifestyle.

French existentialism in this period enjoyed – indeed it still
enjoys – more public recognition and success than any other set
of ideas in the history of modern European philosophy, apart
from Marxism. No doubt it helped that its major representa-
tives – Beauvoir and Sartre – were fascinating and charismatic
figures with an extremely unconventional relationship about
which they spoke quite openly. But the wide distribution of
existentialist ideas was not an accident of publicity or a side-
effect of people's interest in the two philosophers' private lives.
Beauvoir and Sartre deliberately sought to engage as wide a
public as possible, and the forms in which their ideas were
presented and circulated were part of this aim. By 1945
Beauvoir was convinced that the writer's job was to 'understand
her epoch' and address herself directly to her fellow human

beings. (*Force of Circumstance*, p.12) For Beauvoir this meant that the writer's aim was to achieve 'an original grasping of meta-physical reality' ('Literature and Metaphysics', p.273), where metaphysical reality means the non-empirical truth of human existence.

If this means that the writer's aim is basically philosophical, it does not mean that it is necessary to present 'metaphysical real-ity' in the form of a more or less traditional philosophical treatise – as Sartre did, for example, in his *Being and Nothingness*. According to Beauvoir, no single form of writing was in itself better suited than others to this task. In and around 1945, how-ever, Beauvoir most frequently employed one particular form of writing – the journalistic-philosophical essay. The choice of this form was dictated by historical and social circumstances. It was, Beauvoir wrote, 'a groping, seething period of renascence' (*Force of Circumstance*, p.56) in which new problems and challenges presented themselves almost every day. Avenging, justifying or otherwise coming to terms with the immediate collaborationist past and speculating on a radically open future, Beauvoir and her associates were loud voices in a general storm of ideas. Decisions had to be made and positions taken in a broiling atmosphere of urgency. The context demanded a quick and flexible form of writing and publication: a review comprising several short essays in each issue was the obvious vehicle. Writing in this form, for this kind of publication, it is possible, according to Beauvoir, 'to catch the news on the wing, to address one's friends and refute one's adversaries almost as quickly as in private correspondence. I would read an article that made me angry and say to myself immediately: "I must answer that!" That's how all the essays I wrote for *Les temps modernes* came into being.' (*Force of Circumstance*, p.56)

Indeed, that it is how *Les temps modernes* itself came into being. Beauvoir and Sartre founded the review, according to Beauvoir, because the existing reviews were 'inadequate to express the age we were living in'. (*Force of Circumstance*, p.21) With an editorial

committee that included some of the most important French intellectuals of the time – the philosopher Maurice Merleau-Ponty,
the political theorist Raymond Aron, and the writer and poet
Michel Leiris, to name but three – *Les temps modernes* was formed
to fill this gap. Its title, inspired by the Charlie Chaplin film of
the same name (*Modern Times*) was meant to indicate that, in
its attempt to 'express the age', every form of cultural product,
every social expression, however 'low' or insignificant from the
point of view of traditional philosophy, would be worked over in
an attempt to grasp 'metaphysical reality'.

The essay from which this chapter's extract is taken – 'An Eye
for an Eye' – is exemplary both of the journalistic-philosophical
essay form and the content of *Les temps modernes* at this time. The
essay was written in response to the trial and execution of
Robert Brassilach, who, in the pages of a fascist newspaper, had
denounced opponents of the wartime collaborationist government – singling out individuals – and had not just accepted but
actively promoted the anti-Semitism of the occupying powers. A
few days before Brassilach's post-war trial Beauvoir was shocked
to be asked to add her name to those of other writers declaring,
in a petition for clemency for Brasillach, their solidarity with him
as a writer.

In 'An Eye for an Eye' Beauvoir explains why she refused to
sign the petition. In brief, it was because she believed that
Brassilach's decisions were freely taken and could not therefore
be excused by an appeal to any external circumstance (personal
or historical), and because the enormity of his crimes demanded
punishment. He had accomplished the 'absolute evil' of deliberately degrading human beings, an 'abomination' for which 'no
indulgences are permitted.' ('An Eye for an Eye', p.257) To let
this crime go unpunished would be to assent to Brassilach's
abomination. But the justification of Beauvoir's decision is not
the main theme of 'An Eye for an Eye' as it was not the decision
itself that troubled her. Rather, it was that, without overestimat-
ing her role in the outcome of Brassilach's trial and his

subsequent execution, she understood that with this gesture she bore part of the collective responsibility for it.

This acknowledgement of responsibility is not unexpected in the context of existentialist philosophy. More interesting, however, is the stress on the collective nature of the responsibility. The 'we' of this extract is not the formal 'we' of literary style but a true plural: we – Beauvoir and her peers – who had previously held themselves aloof from the apparatus and execution of justice. The 'we' functions in this essay as an effective rebuke to the individualism that Beauvoir herself was to see as one of the major failures of *Pyrrhus and Cineas* and *The Ethics of Ambiguity*. If the sovereign subject eulogized in those works always defined itself against 'public opinion', 'An Eye for An Eye' sees that 'we' are part of it. Previously, Beauvoir says, we enjoyed the luxury of a certain liberal response to crime and criminal justice. We saw the 'assassins and thieves' denounced by society as victims of a social and political order that offered them little alternative to crime and we distanced ourselves from the judicial apparatus of state that judged them and perpetuated this order. These crimes, Beauvoir says, did not compromise any of our values; indeed (it is implied) we felt common cause with them. But now the criminals are war criminals, informers and collaborators: 'Their crimes have struck at our own hearts.' As our values are affirmed by their punishment we find ourselves complicit with the punishing state apparatus. As we have desired the guilty verdicts, and as ours is the public opinion that the courts seek to appease, they are condemned and judged in our name.

As well as explaining this transformation of opinion in relation to the apparatus of justice, it is important that Beauvoir also writes here of the 'poisonous sentiments' that bloomed for the first time in 'our' hearts. We have learned, she says, 'to rage and hate',[5] and we assumed with enthusiasm the role of would-be executioner. If 'vengeance and expiation had no meaning for us before the war,' they now became our dearest wish and held out the promise of 'a joy so heavy that we could scarcely believe ourselves able to bear it'. And yet, Beauvoir says, the joy has not risen up in our hearts. Why has 'a revenge so eagerly desired . . . left this taste of ashes in our mouths'? More particularly, why was Brasillach's death not the joy it once promised to be? Why, on leaving the courtroom after his trial did Beauvoir no longer desire his death? How had it come about that Beauvoir's rage was transformed into the fact that she 'could not envision without anguish that an affirmation of the principle "one must punish traitors" should lead one gray morning to the flowing of real blood'? ('An Eye for an Eye', p.257)

In contemplating these events – the transformation from detached critic to vengeful executioner and then to uneasy accomplice – it is the idea of punishment itself that is at issue. In trying to understand the basis of the need for punishment and assessing the possibility of its satisfaction, Beauvoir's essay moves onto speculative philosophical ground. According to Beauvoir, vengeance (which at this point she does not distinguish from punishment), expressly aims at inflicting suffering or death on its victim – it does not have a primarily practical or utilitarian purpose. Vengeance, she says, 'is not justified by realistic considerations': Mussolini was not killed to deter future dictators. The '"barberings", lynching of snipers, summary execution of certain of the collaborationist police' that followed the liberation were punishments that had no goal outside of themselves. ('Eye for an Eye', p.248) Instead vengeance 'answers a need so deep that it can hold practical requirements in check', as the Treaty of Versailles perhaps shows (the need for vengeance against Germany overrode the requirement for 'a lasting equilibrium in Europe'). Vengeance, Beauvoir writes, 'answers to one of the metaphysical requirements of man'. ('An Eye for an Eye', p.247)

According to Beauvoir, an 'abomination' occurs when, 'by torture, humiliation, servitude, assassination', one human being reduces another to an object and thus denies their existence as a human being. ('An Eye for an Eye', p.248) Such an abomination immediately demands vengeance. Vengeance aims to re-establish the reciprocity between human consciousnesses; that is, it aims to force the abominator to recognize the previously denied freedom – and therefore the human existence – of the victim. Thus, Beauvoir says, 'The affirmation of the reciprocity of interhuman relations is the metaphysical basis of the idea of justice.' ('An Eye for an Eye', p.49)

This is a complex claim. Contrary to the popular idea of justice as a practical requirement, Beauvoir claims that it is a demand that springs from the inherently social nature of human existence. Here, as elsewhere in her philosophical work and novels, Beauvoir aligns herself with Hegel's philosophy. In his *Phenomenology of Spirit*, Hegel tried (successfully, in many people's eyes) to establish the truth that self-consciousness is dependent on the recognition of another self-consciousness. In the simplest terms this means that one's sense of one's self as being a person, a free subject (rather than nothing, or merely an object) is dependent on one's being recognized as such by another. The refusal of this recognition (in the history of slavery and racism; in the everyday refusal of the passerby to acknowledge the existence of the beggar; in the concentration camps and in Abu Ghraib) results in what the historian and theorist Orlando Patterson called 'social death': one's effective exclusion from the community of human beings.[6] In Beauvoir's version of Hegel's claim, the 'reciprocity of interhuman relations' is the *metaphysical* basis of the idea of punishment because it grounds it in the very structure of human being. Vengeance is sought because human existence itself is threatened or denied in abomination or absolute evil, and must be reaffirmed against it.

This view has two important consequences, although Beauvoir does not draw them out here. First, it shows that human existence – the very *being* of human being – is not something given but something constantly to be won anew through affirmation. Second, if the reaffirmation of 'the reciprocity of interhuman existence' is a metaphysical need – the need to affirm ourselves in our being – it is also the basis of morality, of our ethical relations with others. Morality *is* ultimately that reaffirmation. This is very different to, and altogether more sophisticated than, the individualist ethics of *Pyrrhus and Cineas* and *The Ethics of Ambiguity*. Although, like all philosophers, Beauvoir draws on the ideas of her predecessors and contemporaries, her originality here – as elsewhere – is in their bold combination and application. Bringing together Hegel, existentialism and various anthropological studies of vengeance and sacrifice, Beauvoir develops an original philosophical conception of justice out of her reflections on a contemporary case. This is her distinctiveness as a philosophical writer in this period – her ability to show how philosophy lives in the everyday world, or how the everyday world is one that we are able to understand philosophically.

This extract from 'An Eye for an Eye' ends with two questions, which the rest of the essay seeks to answer. First, is the need for punishment well founded? As we have seen, showing that the need for punishment is grounded in the ontological structure of human existence, and that it is thus a 'metaphysical' (or even 'spiritual') need, Beauvoir gives us an affirmative answer. But second, can the need for punishment be satisfied? Does vengeance achieve what it intends? In addressing this question Beauvoir now distinguishes between vengeance proper – 'where the victim takes revenge on his own account' ('An Eye for an Eye', p.250) – and social justice or legally sanctioned punishment. Vengeance, she says, 'is a concrete relation among individuals in the same way that struggle, love, torture, murder or friendship are'. ('An Eye for an Eye', p.251) In vengeance the punishment is attached to the wrong through this concrete relation and only 'vengeance founded on hatred realizes a real reversal of the situation it rejects. Only it bites into the world.' ('An Eye for an Eye', p.258) The implication at this point is that vengeance – hate-fuelled and hot-blooded – does satisfy the metaphysical need of the victim and is thus justified even though it is outside the conventions of law and morality.

Social justice, on the other hand, is not a concrete relation between individuals but a reflective, institutionalized practice that aims to punish without hate in the name of abstract universal principles (thou shalt not murder, and so on). Social justice 'does not engage in a metaphysical struggle with a free consciousness in a body of flesh and blood'. It is the symbolic enactment of society's attempt 'to uphold the values that the crime has negated'. This is clear in the figure of the judge in her wig and gown, and in the ceremonial of the courts and its paraphernalia. The problem is that this symbolic show ends, not symbolically, but with the concrete event of death. The more ceremonial the trial, Beauvoir says, 'the more abominable it seems that it might end in a real spilling of blood'. ('An Eye for an Eye', p.254) In this context the accused takes on a symbolic role and 'is never far from appearing as an expiatory victim'. ('An Eye for an Eye', p.252) The metaphysical need for revenge, filtered through third parties and dispassionate laws, thus fails to be satisfied in social justice because in it punishment 'loses its [metaphysical] signification and its concrete hold on the world'. ('An Eye for an Eye', p.258)

We can understand why, on leaving the courtroom, Beauvoir no longer desired the death of the man whose articles once made her weep with rage, and why 'the joy has not risen up in our hearts', why 'a revenge so eagerly desired has left this taste of ashes in our mouths'. 'Official justice' robs us of the opportunity for vengeance and the wished-for death of the abominator appears, in the guise of state-sanctioned execution, as 'but an arbitrarily imposed penalty'. ('An Eye for an Eye', p.254) Capital punishment, ironically, makes 'us' feel guilty.

The distinction between vengeance and social justice does not long hide Beauvoir's ultimate conclusion: *all* punishment is a failure. Vengeance too fails to achieve the reaffirmation of reciprocity because, in aiming to force the torturer to recognize the freedom he once denied, it pretends to be able to force a free act (for if the torturer does not freely recognize the humanity of his victim the vengeance is hollow). All the same, there was probably some satisfaction in the 'massacres of the S.S. prison guards by their freed captives' ('An Eye for an Eye', p.248), a satisfaction that Beauvoir does not feel in the execution of Robert Brasillach. The question with which 'An Eye for an Eye' really struggles is this: if Brasillach's execution did not satisfy the metaphysical requirement for the re-establishment of reciprocity, was it therefore wrong? Is the standpoint of what Beauvoir calls 'charity' – the standpoint of those who signed the petition for clemency – revealed to be the correct one in the light of Beauvoir's philosophical analysis? In the face of her own distress at the outcome of Brasillach's trial, and despite not being able to 'envision without anguish that an affirmation of the principle "one must punish traitors" should lead one gray morning to the flowing of real blood' – Brasillach's blood – Beauvoir ends her essay with the claim that the inevitable 'failure' of punishment should not stop us punishing: 'For to punish is to recognize man as free in evil as well as in good. It is to distinguish evil from good in the use that man makes of his freedom. It is to will the good.' ('An Eye for an Eye', p.259) If the application of this principle leads to an ambiguous or contradictory situation – I do not wish him dead and yet I believe he must die – we should not be surprised, given the fundamental ambiguity of all action and decision, or the fundamental ambiguity of human existence itself. Perhaps, too, we had to wait for 'An Eye for an Eye' to really understand what might be 'tragic' about this ambiguity.

'An Eye for an Eye' blends philosophical speculation with concrete social commentary in a brilliant demonstration of the way in which each informs and enriches the other. It shows that Beauvoir's aim to achieve 'an original grasping of metaphysical reality' is not the abstruse enterprise that it might first appear, but the desire to understand the profound truth in the concrete realities of everyday life. Otherwise put, 'metaphysical reality' is an everyday thing, and it is in being able to communicate this in accessible forms that the appeal of Beauvoir's existentialism is to be found.

4

BAD FAITH

America is idealistic. In its schools, its churches, its courts, its newspapers, its politicians' speeches, in the text of its laws as well as in private conversations, throughout every region, among all classes, the same credo is affirmed: the one inscribed in the Declaration of Independence and in the preamble to the constitution. It posits the essential dignity of human beings, the basic equality of all men, and certain inalienable rights to liberty, justice, and concrete opportunities for success . . .

Now this credo, so deeply embedded in the heart of all whites, even those in the South, is flagrantly contradicted by the situation of blacks. No one claims that their conditions or opportunities are equal to those of whites. The very fact that blacks sense the injustice done to them and express that with growing strength prevents whites from forgetting it easily. Southerners readily say that there is no black problem, that it's a myth invented by northerners: in fact, they're obsessed with it. The bad faith they bring to discussions is proof itself of the conflict of values going on inside them. Their ignorance helps them; they claim to 'know' the black man, just as French colonials believe they 'know' the native, because their servants are blacks. In fact, their relations with them are utterly false, and they don't try to inform themselves about the real conditions of their servants' lives. But this ignorance could never be great enough to allow them peace of mind. They need other defences. There's an entire system of rationalization engendered in the South, which is also more or less widespread in the North, and its whole purpose is to escape the American dilemma.

The surest way to succeed is to convince oneself that the inequality between blacks and whites is not created by human will but merely confirms a given fact. It is asserted that certain racial characteristics exist that give blacks a lower rank than whites on the biological scale. Usually, certain specific physiological features distinguish blacks from whites. That's clear. But that these features imply inferiority is an unfounded assumption ... Generally, social and biological sciences today tend to view physiological and psychological variations as depending on the setting in which the individual develops, not on fixed hereditary factors. In the last twenty years there hasn't been a single serious work that dared to defend the prejudice, however commonplace, of biological inferiority.

But many racists, ignoring the rigors of science, insist on declaring that even if the physiological reasons haven't been established, the fact is that blacks *are* inferior to whites. You only have to travel through America to be convinced of it. But what does the verb 'to be' mean? Does it define an immutable substance, like oxygen? Or does it describe a moment in a situation that *has evolved*, like every human situation? That is the question.

America Day by Day, pp.235–37.

In January 1947 Beauvoir embarked on a four-month trip to the United States that changed her work and life. The trip was funded by the French Government's Office of Cultural Relations and by various lecture engagements at American universities. Although her engagements determined the basic itinerary, Beauvoir was delighted that it left her 'enormous room for chance and invention' (*Force of Circumstance*, p.132) and she travelled widely in the North and the South, and on both East and West coasts. By this time Beauvoir was sufficiently well known to attract the attention of intellectuals and gossip columnists alike. She became good friends with the writer Richard Wright and his wife Ellen, who introduced her to their circle. At most points in her journey contacts supplied by her new friends and acquaintances were willing to show her around the cities and beyond, although she was quite as happy roaming aimlessly on her own. In Chicago her guide – who showed her the city's 'lower depths' (*America Day by Day*, p.105) – was the writer Nelson Algren, with whom Beauvoir had a passionate love affair and, she said, the best sex of her life. In the next few years Beauvoir returned several times to Chicago to be with Algren, and they travelled together, notably in Mexico.

By January 1948 Beauvoir had retrospectively constructed a journal of her first trip to the States, later published as *America Day by Day*. The form of this book is interesting because it is internally complex, written from 'notes, letters, and memories that were still fresh' (*America Day by Day*, p.15), and presented in the form of a transcribed diary. It blends straight reportage, including statistics (on demographics and education, for example), with historical background, personal impressions and experiences and socio-cultural criticism. In her autobiography and her letters to Algren, Beauvoir refers to it as 'a book about America' (*Force of Circumstance*, p.131), but it is equally a book about Beauvoir herself. Indeed, Beauvoir wrote nothing that was not personal. This may to some extent be true of most writing, however 'objective' its apparent form, but it was raised to the level of a conscious principle in Beauvoir's work. As the world only reveals itself to individual consciousnesses, it could not be thought, according to Beauvoir, that the point of view of the individual is a distortion of an objective reality independent of subjectivity. On the contrary, it is pretending otherwise, and disavowing the subjective element in writing, that leads to distortion.

In the Preface to *America Day by Day* Beauvoir stresses the impressionistic and partial nature of her observations on American life, insisting that 'no isolated piece represents a definitive judgment'. Its value, however, lies precisely in these features: 'it is truthful only because it includes the unique personal circumstances in which each discovery was made'. (*America Day by Day*, p.15) And, indeed, the first person viewpoint allows Beauvoir to present some of the objective realities of American life with great power. On first encountering segregated restrooms and restaurants in Texas, and noting the 'wretched' state of those reserved for blacks, Beauvoir wrote:

> we understand we've crossed a frontier . . .This is the first time we see with our own eyes the segregation that we've heard so much about. And although we'd been warned, something fell onto our shoulders that would not lift all through the South; it was our own skin that became heavy and stifling, its color making us burn. (*America Day by Day*, p.204)[7]

This remark ends the entry for 25 March; no more is said about it that day. It is as if the enormity of the realities of Southern racism leaves Beauvoir temporarily struck dumb. As the topic is picked up in the entries for the following days Beauvoir intersperses an almost dispassionate description of the contrast between white wealth and black poverty with historical and economic analysis evidently based on research conducted after the trip. The descriptive passages are extremely successful in evoking atmosphere and the uncomfortable mood of the travellers:

> Suddenly, without realizing it, we find ourselves in the black section. Peeling wooden houses stand amid lots overgrown with weeds and crossed by cracked alleyways. In two spots, black ashes and half-burned boards tell us of recent fires. The streets are empty. Here and there we see an old black man or a fat matron swinging on one of those moving veranda chairs. Children

are gathered around a kiosk selling Coca-Cola, bananas, and
candy. A voice from an invisible phonograph drifts out and is lost
among the weeds, the ashes and the silence. Two or three blacks
pass by without acknowledging us. (*America Day by Day*, p.209)

In New Orleans, refused a ride by black cab drivers – it was illegal for black drivers to carry white passengers, but the refusals
were also acts of vengeance – Beauvoir and her companions 'go
by foot across this enemy territory, this part of town where we
are the enemy despite ourselves, responsible for the color of our
skin and all that it implies'. (*America Day by Day*, p.228)

As Beauvoir travelled further in the South the entries dwell
more and more – and for a while exclusively – on segregation
and racism: 'the great tragedy of the South pursues us like an
obsession'. (*America Day by Day*, p.231) In the entry for 3 April
Beauvoir begins the psycho-philosophical analysis of white
racism from which this chapter's extract is taken. On her first
evening in New York, she recounts, a Frenchman asked her not
to write anything about 'the black question, on the pretext that
I couldn't understand anything in only three months'. (*America
Day by Day*, p.234) Although we do not know what she replied
then, by this time the answer is obvious: how could she *not*
write anything about it? Admitting that her experience was still
meagre (although, how much experience of the mere fact of segregation does one need?) Beauvoir refers us to Gunnar Myrdal's
1944 study of 'the black problem', *The American Dilemma: The
Negro Problem and Modern Democracy*, as her major source.

Myrdal's book, based on research conducted between 1938
and 1942, is one of the most famous and influential early sociological studies of what we would now call 'race relations' in the
United States. The 'American dilemma' is the ugly contradiction
between the American 'credo', described by Beauvoir in this
extract from *America Day by Day*, and 'the situation of the
blacks'. Beauvoir immediately entwines this 'flagrant contradiction' with others, less obvious perhaps but no less important. No

one, black or white, would deny that black Americans do not
enjoy conditions or opportunities equal to their white compa-
triots, and yet the white Southerners claim there is really no
problem. They claim to 'know' the black man – both 'what' he
is and how he lives – and yet they are ignorant and do not try to
remedy their ignorance. This willed ignorance, Beauvoir says, is
not enough to bring the white Southerners peace of mind, not
enough to overcome the contradictions and 'the conflict of
values going on inside them'. Thus 'an entire system of rationalization' is required to defend themselves against this inner
conflict, and this system of rationalization – the racist ideology
that justifies inequality and segregation – is the form of the 'bad
faith' which, according to Beauvoir, accompanies all their discussions of the problem.

With the introduction here of the notion of 'bad faith',
Beauvoir seamlessly blends Myrdal's sociological analysis with
her own existentialism. 'Bad faith' is a central theme in Sartre's
Being and Nothingness, where the category received its first
extended philosophical treatment. Its meaning is dependent on
the account of human existence largely shared by Sartre and
Beauvoir. In Sartre's version, as radically free beings (free in the
metaphysical sense), we bear the whole burden of responsibility
for our choices, whether trivial or momentous, and whatever the
conditions under which they are made. This undoubtedly
extreme position is more persuasive than it may first appear. For
although we might be tempted to think that under certain conditions our choices and actions are compelled by external factors,
thus mitigating our responsibility for them, simple examples can
show why we need not think this. If, for instance, with a gun to
my head, I am forced to hand over my bag to an attacker, I nevertheless do this freely, as I could have chosen to do otherwise. I
could, for example, have refused (although, given the probabil-
ity of that choice leading to injury or death, it would have been
a foolish choice). Conceding that I freely gave my bag to the
mugger does not make me guilty or responsible for the attack, it

just means I chose rationally in a bad situation. But Sartre believed – and a moment of honest introspection on any given issue might confirm it to us – that most of the time we would rather pretend that we do not bear the responsibility for our choices, especially to the extent that this means we must bear the responsibility for who we are. When, instead of acknowledging our freedom and responsibility, we find excuses or other explanations for our choices, we are in 'bad faith'. Bad faith is thus a kind of lying to oneself.

Beauvoir's skill in bringing philosophy down to earth is illustrated in her application of the concept of bad faith to the analysis of Southern racism. Racist Southerners are in bad faith, according to Beauvoir, because they refuse to accept responsibility for the situation of the blacks. Historically, it was white traders who brought black slaves to America and racial inequality – economic and social – is the legacy of this slavery. More importantly, it is the white population that perpetuates the situation today. The specific form of their bad faith is the denial that the situation is the outcome of human will. They see it, Beauvoir says, as the confirmation of a given fact: the natural inferiority of black people in relation to white people, that is, in relation to themselves. This biological racism – for which there is no scientific evidence – seeks to justify itself by appealing to what Beauvoir is content to acknowledge as fact: physiological differences between human beings. But the racist assumption that these undeniable physiological differences imply a relationship of inferiority and superiority is false, because unfounded. Beauvoir goes on to claim a biological and social scientific consensus for the view that physiological and psychological variations are environmentally, not hereditarily, determined. We can thus identify two separate questions to which this extract gives rise. First, how is it that physiological differences come to be interpreted, by the racist, in terms of inferiority and superiority? Second, what accounts for those physiological and psychological differences?

In the last paragraph of the extract it becomes clear that it is – perhaps surprisingly – the second of these questions that concerns Beauvoir. And when we understand what Beauvoir is saying here we may feel extremely uncomfortable with her position. The racist insists, Beauvoir says, 'that even if the physiological reasons haven't been established, the fact is that blacks *are* inferior to whites'. But, Beauvoir asks what does the verb 'to be' mean in the claim that blacks *are* inferior? Does it describe a state of affairs that is fixed, not open to change (as in the statement 'I am a human being'), or does it describe what simply happens to be the case now and which may very well change (as in the statement 'I am hungry')? Beauvoir identifies the bad faith of the racist as their belief that the inferiority of black people is a permanent state of affairs with a biological basis, that it is 'not created by human will', and thus through human history, but 'merely confirms a given fact'. But the truth of the matter, Beauvoir concludes, is that the inferiority of black people is only 'a moment in a situation that *has evolved*, like every human situation'. Beauvoir does not deny that black people are inferior to white people, she denies only that this inferiority is biologically determined and thus not possible to overcome. Bad faith is not the white acceptance of the inferiority of black people, it is the refusal to take responsibility for its socio-historical origin. This is why the question of the cause of racial differences is an important one for Beauvoir.

Considered alone, the philosophical form of Beauvoir's argument here is unimpeachable. It rests on her existentialist sensitivity to the semantic multiplicity of the verb 'to be'. The increasing complexity of this sensitivity in Beauvoir's later work in relation to other topics is the basis of some of her most original thought. But the premises of the argument are confused and highly questionable. Beauvoir's analysis in this extract moves from a discussion of economic and social inequality to one of racial inferiority because belief in the latter, with an alleged biological justification, is the form of the racist bad faith with which the whites in her discussion try to convince themselves of the naturalness of the situation. Nothing justifies Beauvoir's subsequent acceptance of the 'fact' of this inferiority, which becomes the major premise in her argument. With her existentialist philosophical framework, we might rather have expected Beauvoir to talk about the *interpretation of* existing physiological differences in terms of inferiority and superiority (a discussion in which the origin of those differences would be irrelevant) or to point out the mistake involved in the use of the value judgements 'inferior' and 'superior' to name alleged properties of human beings, as if to 'confirm a given fact'. That is, the value judgements 'inferior' and 'superior' belong to the one making the judgement, they are not objective qualities of that which is judged. Instead of identifying this as another aspect of the bad faith of racism, Beauvoir guilelessly reveals her own bad faith in the matter.

There is, however, a huge difference between the bad faith of the Southern racism that Beauvoir discusses and her own. The former emerges in the context of self-justification as a defence mechanism designed to relieve the racist of the burden not just of responsibility but also of self-reflection. The latter, on the other hand, emerges in the context of Beauvoir's reflective examination of her own position in a racist society. Although she could have affected a disinterested stance and claimed that, as an outsider in America, she was merely an external observer of its race relations, she acknowledges that she has become a part of it in her travels through the South: 'we are the enemy despite ourselves, responsible for the colour of our skin and all that it implies.' Painfully aware of the privilege she enjoyed as a white woman in the South, Beauvoir attempted to transgress the racial divide several times – she visited a black dancehall in New Orleans, for example – but she found that the goodwill of a European intellectual does not miraculously part the waters of hate or cut a swathe through the immense socio-historical weight of racism and segregation.

The blunt introduction of the discussion of segregation and its carefully escalating presence in *America Day by Day* bears witness to the hesitancy with which Beauvoir broached a subject of which she previously knew very little, but of which her limited experience was intense. Her decision that the importance of the experience outweighed her lack of knowledge, shows how the personal element in experience may yet reveal what has most objective weight. And we can now see that the Frenchman's plea in New York – don't write about 'the black question'; you can't possibly know anything about it in only three months – was an invitation to bad faith. You can absolve yourself of the decision not to write about it, he seemed to say, by claiming that circumstances make it impossible for you to write about it – you can say you don't know enough. It was to her great credit that she refused and thus exposed herself to the criticisms of subsequent generations.

5

'WOMAN'

First we must ask: what is a woman? '*Tota mulier in utero*', says one, woman is her womb. But in speaking of certain women, connoisseurs declare that they are not women, although they are equipped with a uterus like the rest. All agree in recognizing the fact that females exist in the human species: today, as always, they make up about one half of humanity. And yet we are told that femininity is in danger; we are exhorted to be women, remain women, become women. It would appear, then, that every female human being is not necessarily a woman; to be so considered she must share in that mysterious and threatened reality known as femininity. Is this attribute something secreted by the ovaries? Or is it a Platonic essence, a product of the philosophic imagination? Is a rustling petticoat enough to bring it down to earth? . . .

The biological and social sciences no longer admit the existence of unchangeably fixed entities that determine given characteristics, such as those ascribed to woman, the Jew or the Negro. Science regards any characteristic as a reaction dependent in part upon a *situation*. If today femininity no longer exists, then it never existed. But does the word *woman*, then have no specific content? This is stoutly affirmed by those who hold to the philosophy of the Enlightenment, of rationalism, of nominalism;

women, to them, are merely the human beings arbitrarily designated by the word *woman* . . .

But nominalism is a rather inadequate doctrine, and the anti-feminists have had no trouble in showing that women simply *are not* men. Surely woman is, like man, a human being; but such a declaration is abstract. The fact is that every concrete human being is always a singular, separate individual. To decline to accept such notions as the eternal feminine, the black soul, the Jewish character, is not to deny that Jews, Negroes, women exist today . . . In truth to go for a walk with one's eyes open is enough to demonstrate that humanity is divided into two classes of individuals whose clothes, faces, bodies, smiles, gaits, interests, and occupations are manifestly different. Perhaps these differences are superficial, perhaps they are destined to disappear. What is certain is that they do most obviously exist.

If her functioning as a female is not enough to define woman, if we decline also to explain her through 'the eternal feminine', and if nevertheless we admit, provisionally, that women do exist, then we must face the question: what is a woman?

The Second Sex, pp.13–15.[8]

What is a woman? Beauvoir was probably the first Western writer to ask this question seriously and without prejudice, that is, without knowing the answer in advance. In 1946 Beauvoir wanted to write about herself. Mulling over the idea with Sartre a first question posed itself: 'What has it meant to me to be a woman?' And precisely because she had never thought about it before – '"For me," I said to Sartre, "you might almost say that it just hasn't counted"' – her investigation of the question was 'a revelation'. (*Force of Circumstance*, p.103) Abandoning the idea of a personal work, Beauvoir instead went to the Bibilothèque nationale to do some reading, and studied 'the myths of femininity'. It is testament to Beauvoir's incredible capacity for work that only three years later – years during which she also wrote *America Day by Day*, various other essays, and edited

Les temps modernes – the first volume of *The Second Sex* was published.

The Second Sex is, without doubt, one of the most important books of the twentieth century. It was the single most significant text for the feminist movements that helped transform Western societies in the second half of the twentieth century and continues to be read hungrily throughout the world. When Beauvoir died in 1986 thousands marched behind her funeral cortège. Scholars, prominent feminists, delegations from women's groups from across continents, inconspicuous Parisians and sundry admirers piled her grave high with flowers and alarmed the police with their numbers. The French writer and feminist Elizabeth Badinter summed up the feelings of many with her claim, 'Women, you owe everything to her!'[9] Although it took Beauvoir until the 1970s to publicly declare herself a feminist, she spent her last years campaigning on feminist issues, in the defence of women internationally, and was pleased – if still a little surprised – by the inspiration women drew from *The Second Sex*. Marshalling an immense body of historical, anthropological, literary and anecdotal evidence the book describes and analyzes – with great restraint but vicious bite and beautiful wit – the situation of women from pre-history to 1949. Book One, 'Facts and Myths', considers woman as object in a dual sense: the object of historical research and the object constructed through (male) myth and fantasy. Book Two, 'Lived Experience', describes the world in which women find themselves from their own point of view, as subjects. One fundamental issue emerges again and again: what are the limits – physical, economic, social, psychological – that constrain women's freedom, and can they be overcome?

In *The Second Sex* Beauvoir was fearless. She covered topics that her bourgeois contemporaries professed to find scandalous (for example, abortion and lesbianism) and incurred their sanctimonious wrath for writing with clear-eyed honesty – instead of sentimentality – about those subjects that they held most dear (motherhood and marriage, in particular). Although the publication of the first volume was in one sense a great success (it sold very well and made Beauvoir famous), Beauvoir was in equal measure reviled and insulted. When extracts were first published in *Les temps modernes* the critical and public reaction was extraordinary:

> What a festival of obscenity on the pretext of flogging me for mine! That good old *esprit gaulois* flowed in torrents. I received – some signed and some anonymous – epigrams, epistles, satires, admonitions, and exhortations addressed to me by, for example, 'some very active members of the First Sex'. Unsatisfied, frigid, priapic, nymphomaniac, lesbian, a hundred times aborted, I was everything, even an unmarried mother. (*Force of Circumstance*, p.197)

This was perhaps to be expected from certain quarters, Beauvoir wrote, but not from the Catholic novelist-poet François Mauriac. 'Your employer's vagina has no secrets from me', he wrote in a private letter to a contributor to *Les temps modernes* after reading extracts from *The Second Sex*, although he probably regretted it when Beauvoir and Sartre published his comments in the next issue.

No doubt the authors of these various attacks were quite sure that they knew perfectly well what a woman was, not least because they were sure that Beauvoir had somehow transgressed the limits of behaviour expected of one. This chapter's extract, taken from the opening paragraphs of the introduction to *The Second Sex*, reveals the confusions and contradictions in the pronouncements of this self-assured presumption. Beauvoir quotes the kinds of things that those who think they know what a woman is might say. Her first point is that these commonplace utterances themselves, each of which presents itself as obviously true, tacitly presume a distinction between two categories – the female and the woman – which they explicitly treat as identical.

For example, the implicit meaning of the idea that 'woman is her womb' is that 'woman' should be understood in purely biological terms. This translates into the everyday assumption that 'woman' is the term for the female of the human species. The distinction between male and female – sex difference – is based on the different roles of each in reproduction. The claim that 'woman is her womb' reduces woman to her reproductive function, implying that she is a merely physical, and not intellectual, entity. And yet, Beauvoir continues, self-proclaimed experts on women (which, unfortunately, France has never lacked) are quite happy to declare of certain women in full possession of a uterus that 'they are not women', or perhaps not 'real' women. If, therefore, there are some females who nevertheless cannot be said to be women, popular opinion itself presumes a distinction between a biological category (female) and an ideological category (woman). Although this distinction is not Beauvoir's theoretical innovation, the philosophical originality of *The Second Sex* lies in her attempt to draw out the truth implicit in it, and in the attempt to answer the question of what it therefore means to be a woman. Beauvoir abandoned the project of the personal confession – 'What has it meant *to me* to be a woman?'– because she realized that this more general treatment was the necessary prelude to it.

If all women are female, but not all females are women, there must be something added to the female who is also a woman. What is this? Beauvoir ridicules the empty notion of 'femininity' that is said to be the mysterious X of womanliness, but the ridicule has a serious point. Although it refers to nothing tangible, the idea of 'femininity' plays a vital role in delimiting acceptable behaviour and expectations for women, which explains why Beauvoir's contemporaries could see its very existence threatened by women's increasing liberation. When Beauvoir says that 'the biological and social sciences no longer believe in the existence of immutably fixed entities determining given characteristics such as those of the woman, the Jew or the

Black' she means that we no longer believe in the idea that mythical entities such as 'femininity', 'the black soul' or 'the Jewish character' are the cause of all the characteristics that typify women, black people or Jews. The alignment of 'woman', 'black' and 'Jew' here is interesting. No doubt the argument in Sartre's 1946 *Réflexions sur la question juive* (translated in 1965 as *Anti-Semite and Jew*) against a determining 'Jewish essence' was influential, and it is well documented that Myrdal's *The American Dilemma* was the model for *The Second Sex*. (In 1947 Beauvoir wrote to Algren that she would like *The Second Sex*, which she was then writing, to be as important as Myrdal's book about the condition of American blacks. *Beloved Chicago Man*, p.116)

Beauvoir's comparison is not entirely successful, mainly because there is no biological category in the case of the Jew or the black person that is equivalent to the category of the female from which the 'woman' is distinguished. It does, however, have the virtue of demonstrating the general scope of this kind of existential analysis. Although her specific topic is 'woman', many of the questions she asks could be asked of other social groups. Indeed, Frantz Fanon's *Black Skin, White Masks* (1952) did undertake a similarly existential analysis of 'the lived experience of the black man'[10], asking what it meant to exist as a black man in racist Europe and its colonies. It is interesting to note that, despite the global influence of *The Second Sex* on the feminist movements of the twentieth and twenty-first centuries, no significant philosophical tradition of specifically existentialist feminism sprang from it. Rather, the feminist philosophy which now takes its cue from Beauvoir is, as we shall see in these chapters on *The Second Sex*, a development of some of her main insights in other directions. However, the tradition of black existentialism, predominantly in the United States, is one of the most important strands in the political legacy of existentialist philosophy.

The most important point in Beauvoir's comparison of woman, black person and Jew is that there is no mysterious determining essence in each case, and that the typical (non-physiological) characteristics are to be understood as a 'reaction to a *situation*'. Thus it is not 'femininity' that makes females into women, it is their situation. The term 'situation' has a specific meaning in existentialist philosophy. It refers to the context of individual human existence within and against which freedom asserts itself. One's situation includes all those aspects of one's existence that one did not choose. Some of these are obvious: for example the conditions of one's birth (place, time, family), or the specific form of one's embodiment (including sex and being able-bodied or disabled). But one's situation also includes one's past – because, although we are responsible for our past, it cannot be changed – and the less easily specifiable conditions of social and cultural existence. It is important that the concepts of situation and freedom are ultimately inseperable in existentialist philosophy. Human freedom, as distinct from the omnipotence of a god, is only realized in its relation to situation. The situation is like the resistance of the air that allows the bird to fly. Conversely, it is only meaningful to speak of a situation for a free being, or a situation is only revealed as such in its relation to freedom.

Sartre and Beauvoir shared this conception of 'freedom in situation', but disagreed on one crucial point. For Sartre, no situation could ever make any difference to the absolute nature of human freedom. No matter how constrained one's physical or social freedoms were, in the worst situations imaginable, the *ontological* freedom that is human being could never be compromised. Although Beauvoir did not go so far as to argue that ontological freedom could be annihilated or completely suppressed (given her definition of the human as freedom, how could she?), she disagreed with Sartre in placing much more emphasis on the weight of the situation in existentialist analysis.[11] This is one of her most important contributions to existentialist philosophy, and one which commentators have found difficult to argue against. Beauvoir claimed that there were some situations (slavery, for example) in relation to which talk of ontological freedom was otiose, or worse. Also, unlike Sartre, Beauvoir afforded the situation an explanatory value, as this extract from *The Second Sex* shows. It is to the situation that we must look to understand what makes the human female into a woman.

But if the notion of the situation gives us the context in which a human female can become a woman, it still does not answer the opening (and closing) question of this extract: what is a woman? In order to understand what is at stake in this question we need to return to the more fundamental question that Beauvoir had asked in *America Day by Day*: 'what does the verb "to be" mean?' Although there is little or no explicit reference to it in *The Second Sex*, the presumption of the importance of this question in existentialist philosophy is due to the influence of the German philosopher Martin Heidegger. In his best-known work, *Being and Time* (1927), Heidegger pointed out that although, in all Indo-European languages, variants of the verb 'to be' provide us with perhaps the most indispensable element of language, which of us can say what the little word 'be' actually means? Of course we all understand phrases in which parts of the verb are used ('it is raining'; 'I am sad'; 'is this OK?'; 'how are you?'), but this makes it all the more remarkable, according to Heidegger, that we can nevertheless not say what 'being' means. Furthermore, any enquiry into the meaning of being is beset with circularity, as the question 'What is the meaning of being?' already presupposes an understanding of being in our use of the word 'is'.

According to Heidegger, the difficulties of approaching the question of the meaning of being are such that we can only begin by asking questions about what 'being' means in relation to one particular kind of entity: ourselves.[12] Heidegger reserved the term 'existence' (*Existenz*) for the being of the entity that we ourselves are and called the enquiry into its fundamental characteristics 'existential analysis', the philosophical model for Beauvoir's and Sartre's existentialism. Although, for Heidegger, existential analysis was only to be a step on the way to the under-

standing of being as such (what he called 'fundamental ontology'), for Beauvoir and Sartre existential analysis was an end in
itself.

One of the first claims in Heidegger's *Being and Time* is the
insistence on the difference between the being of that kind of entity
that we ourselves are – human existence, in Beauvoir's terms –
and the being of other kinds of entity, for example the kinds of
entities that chairs and tables are. Although this ontological difference may seem obvious, it was Heidegger's contention that the
history of philosophy and the discourses based on it (that is, all
discourses, as far as Heidegger was concerned) were disfigured by
the constant mistaken tendency to think of human existence in
terms that were inappropriate to it, in terms only appropriate
to things like tables and chairs. Simply put, this means that the
fundamental mistake of philosophy and the social and human
sciences is that they tend to talk of human beings as if they are
things like tables and chairs, albeit vastly more complicated. *Being
and Time*, on the other hand, is an attempt to think human
existence in the unique terms appropriate to it, that is, precisely,
to think about it existentially.

Beauvoir takes this philosophical background for granted.
Thus the question 'what is a woman?' is not a question like
'what is a chair?' or 'what is a table?' It does not ask us to list the
attributes or characteristics that together make up that thing
called a 'woman'. It does not ask us to provide a definition of the
word 'woman'. It asks: what is it to exist *as a woman*? What difference does it make to human existence when that human
existence is the existence of a woman? It is an *existential* question.
But with this Beauvoir goes far beyond, and implicitly criticizes,
the philosophy that was her inspiration. For Heidegger – and following him, for Sartre too – human existence was conceived in
abstraction from the fact that, as Beauvoir says, 'humanity is
divided into two classes of individuals', man and woman. For
Heidegger this division was not fundamental; for Sartre it could
make no difference to the ontological freedom of the human and

did not figure as an object of analysis in his philosophy. On the evidence of this extract, we would have to conclude that Heidegger's and Sartre's analyses – and indeed her own earlier work – were, for Beauvoir, guilty to some extent of the same vitiating abstraction as 'the partisans of Enlightenment philosophy, of rationalism and nominalism' that she criticizes in the extract above for their overly generalized concept of humanity.

Although Beauvoir insists on the importance of the distinction between men and women in existential analysis, the conceptual distinction between the female and the woman always serves to remind us that 'men' and 'women' are categories that remain to be elucidated. 'Man' and 'woman' are not simply different terms for the sexual division of male and female, not least because, according to Beauvoir, the latter *are* identifiable by virtue of the possession of certain attributes: 'male' and 'female' are *defined by* their different functions in reproduction. We should note, furthermore, that the obviousness of the distinction between men and women is illustrated here by a rather curious set of signs ('the clothes, the face, the body, the smiles, the gait, the interests and the occupations'), and the status of these differences is immediately called in to question. Despite the introduction of the category of the situation, this extract gives us no answer to its basic question – what is a woman? – but, rather, insistently reasserts the philosophical pertinence of it. In so doing, these passages from *The Second Sex* are the inauguration of an entirely novel field: the philosophical analysis of sex and gender. More than fifty years after their first publication, the full implications of Beauvoir's innovation have yet to be understood.

6

OTHER

What is a woman? . . .

The fact that I ask it is in itself significant. A man would never set out to write a book on the peculiar situation of the human male. But if I wish to define myself, I must first of all say: 'I am a woman'; on this truth must be based all further discussion. A man never begins by presenting himself as an individual of a certain sex; it goes without saying that he is a man. The terms *masculine* and *feminine* are used symmetrically only as a matter of form, as on legal papers. In actuality the relation of the two sexes is not quite like that of two electrical poles, for man represents both the positive and the neutral, as is indicated by the common use of *man* to designate human beings in general . . . woman represents only the negative, defined by limiting criteria, without reciprocity. In the midst of an abstract discussion it is vexing to hear a man say: 'You think thus and so because you are a woman'; but I know my only defence is to reply: 'I think thus and so because it is true,' thereby removing my subjective self from the argument. It would be out of the question to reply: 'And you think the contrary because you are a man', for it is understood that the fact of being a man is no peculiarity. A man is in the right in being a man; it is the woman who is in the wrong. It amounts to this: just as for the ancients there was an absolute vertical with reference to which the oblique was defined, so there is an absolute human type, the masculine . . . 'The female is a female by virtue of a certain *lack* of qualities,' said Aristotle; 'we should regard the female nature as afflicted with a natural defectiveness.' And St Thomas for his part pronounced woman to be an 'imperfect' man, an 'incidental' being. This is symbolized in Genesis where Eve is depicted as made from what Bossuet called 'a supernumerary bone' of Adam.

Thus humanity is male and man defines woman not in herself but as relative to him; she is not regarded as an autonomous being . . . And she is simply what man decrees; thus she is called 'the sex', by which is meant that she appears essentially to the male as a sexed being. For him she is sex – absolute sex, no less. She is defined and differentiated with reference to man and not he with reference to her; she is the incidental, the inessential as opposed to the essential. He is the Subject, he is the Absolute – she is the Other.

The Second Sex, pp.15–16.

Although the central philosophical question of *The Second Sex* – what is a woman? – concerns women specifically, it would be a grave misunderstanding to think of it as a book only for women. The tendency to do so stems from the prejudice that 'gender' is a women's issue, rather than a fundamental aspect of the contemporary situation of both men and women. The basic form of Beauvoir's question is equally pertinent in relation to the 'first' sex: what is a man? What is it to exist *as a man*? What difference does it make to human existence when that human existence is the existence of a man? What are the myths of masculinity that prescribe and limit the behaviour of and expectations for men? As girls in Western societies have begun to outperform boys at school, as the traditional masculine role of breadwinner and patriarch has become outmoded, and as the comfort blanket of belief in male superiority has become ridiculous, it is arguably more important to ask these questions today of 'man' than it is of 'woman'. For how else will we stave off the risk of a unreflective retreat into exaggerated pre-feminist forms of masculinity? Perhaps the most important lesson of Beauvoir's analysis is that we bring up our children – boys and girls – with an astonishing blindness if we do not first ask ourselves what it is that we are bringing them up *to be* as men and women.

It is, then, ironic that the first critical reactions to *The Second Sex* failed to acknowledge the general scope of Beauvoir's enquiry, and that their inability to see its relevance to men was predicted and explained in the book. The fact is that although we *could* ask these questions of 'man' – it is a distinct philosophical possibility – we generally *do not*, because the basic structure of the relation between men's and women's situations prevents it.[13] This, in sum, is the main point in this chapter's extract, also taken from the introduction to the first volume of *The Second Sex*.

Beauvoir's opening point refers us back to the origin of *The Second Sex* and Beauvoir's realization that to write about herself required her first to write about what it meant to be a woman. This requirement, it turns out, is double edged. Beauvoir is, she says, obliged to declare that she is a woman, when no man would be obliged to declare his manhood in similar circumstances. Would Sartre have suggested to his male friends that to write about themselves would first have required them to write about what it meant to be a man? Probably not, but this does not mean that he gave Beauvoir bad advice. For this obligation revealed something crucial to Beauvoir: the asymmetry of the *existential* – as well as social and economic – relation between men and women. On the one hand the requirement is experienced as a burden. Whether she likes it or not her being a woman constitutes the ground upon which every other claim must be based. It allows, as a consequence, irritating men to say 'you think thus and so because you are a woman'. On the other hand, the fact of her being a woman *was* one of the most far-reaching aspects of her singular situation and the ability to acknowledge this enabled her to write one of the most important books of the twentieth century. Throughout this extract, and indeed the rest of *The Second Sex*, the ambivalent nature of this obligation is a point of constructive tension.

For Beauvoir, the asymmetry in the distinction between man and woman is constitutive of the meaning of the two terms, but it must be borne in mind continually that Beauvoir is never speaking here of unchangeable essences or 'natural' facts. This asymmetry constitutes what man and woman each *are*, but their being is not fixed. The most obvious form of this asymmetry is linguistic: the use, in diverse languages, of the masculine pronoun or noun to refer, generically, to all human beings, men *and* women. For centuries this has been dismissed as a meaningless linguistic fact, but Beauvoir explains the existential meaning of the use of the generic masculine, and anyone who would deny its pertinence is obliged to answer in these terms. Linguistic usage affirms, according to Beauvoir, that the masculine 'constitutes an absolute human type' that defines the norm against which the non-masculine is measured. In her examples from Western religion, philosophy and literature in the extract above, Beauvoir refers to some well-known proponents of this view. This is not because she believed that many of her contemporaries actually subscribed to these views in the same form, but because they express, in particularly stark terms, the asymmetrical relation of dependence and independence that characterises the different situations of men and women.

The idea that woman is inferior to or derived from man, in whatever sense intended by Genesis or Aristotle, is a form of the idea that man can be thought in his own terms, while woman can only be thought in relation to man. Man is the 'essential' term in the relation between man and woman, and woman is 'inessential'. Man is the substance of the human – where a 'substance' is something that exists independently of anything else – while woman is an 'accident', a philosophical term for something which, in itself, has no independent or self-sufficient existence. In describing the situation of man and woman in these terms (essential/inessential, substance/accident) Beauvoir is mimicking those philosophical discourses that misunderstand and misrepresent human being in terms of a fixed essence or nature. However, to the extent that these philosophical discourses have contributed to the formation of the contemporary situations of men and women, Beauvoir is able to re-describe their effect in existentialist terms: man is the Subject, woman is the Other.

The category of the Other (Beauvoir usually capitalizes the word) is, according to Beauvoir, 'as primordial as consciousness itself'. (*The Second Sex*, p.16) The passages that expand upon this claim are based on an interpretation of aspects of Hegel's philosophy. According to Hegel in his *Phenomenology of Spirit*, a self-conscious being can only recognize itself as such by first being recognized by another self-consciousness. However, this recognition is not simply given, it must be won. This is because, according to Hegel, a second self-consciousness imposes limits on the freedom and desires of the first, and vice versa, resulting in what Hegel called a 'struggle for recognition'. The first resolution of this struggle is set out in Hegel's celebrated 'dialectic of lordship and bondage', otherwise known as the master/slave dialectic. Realising that a dead opponent cannot recognize the victor, one self-consciousness assumes the position of the Lord, forcing the other – in fear for its life – into the position of his Bondsman. However, this is an empty victory for the Lord, who finds no satisfaction in the recognition of the Bondsman's unfree self-consciousness. Indeed, for Hegel, the labour that the Bondsman undertakes on behalf of the Lord offers more satisfaction as the Bondsman recognizes his own self 'objectified' (that is, externalized in the form of an object) in the products of his labour and the way his labour transforms this world. Even so, the Bondsman's position in relation to the Lord is only a stage in a series of transitions to the final outcome of this process: the reciprocal recognition of self-consciousnesses.

Although Hegel uses specific historical-social categories in the account of this dialectic, it is not intended to describe any actual historical event or epoch. After a series of influential lectures by the Russian émigré philosopher Alexandre Kojève in Paris in the 1930s, an existential (as opposed to either an historical or purely conceptual) interpretation of the master/slave dialectic predominated among the French intelligentsia. Hegel's account was taken to be a model for understanding the mutually constitutive relation between self-consciousnesses, between individual human existences. As a result of Kojève's influence on Sartre, the idea of a struggle for recognition is central to the account of human relations in Sartre's *Being and Nothingness*, the text to which Beauvoir was in many ways most indebted. For Sartre the outcome of the struggle could never be reciprocal recognition. According to Sartre, the never-ending struggle could only ever result in the temporary objectification of one consciousness by another in a permanently unstable seesaw or jockeying for position. There was, for Sartre, no possible relation between subject and subject, only between subject and object. From her earliest work, Beauvoir disagreed with this pessimistic – indeed almost autistic – account of human relations. In 'An Eye for An Eye', for example, Beauvoir calls the affirmation of the reciprocal recognition of the other's freedom 'the metaphysical basis of the idea of justice', its negation 'the most fundamental form of injustice'. ('An Eye for an Eye', p.249) In *The Second Sex* Beauvoir accepts that 'we find in consciousness itself a fundamental hostility towards every other consciousness', but nonetheless maintains that 'individuals and groups are obliged to recognize the reciprocity of their relations'. (*The Second Sex*, p.17)

It did not seem to Beauvoir (on this point a better reader of Hegel than was Sartre) that the hostility and inequality of the relation between Bondsman and Lord was the inevitable form of human relations, so the situations of men and women struck her as bizarre and unjust. To be a subject, in Beauvoir's terms, is to posit oneself in opposition to, or in reciprocity with, another subject, as a self-conscious and self-determining freedom. To be the Other is to be posited by another subject as an object with fixed possibilities. This specific concept of the Other is Beauvoir's innovation. (There are concepts of the 'other' in both Hegel's and Sartre's work but neither corresponds precisely to Beauvoir's.) It describes an *existential* degradation, a degrading transformation of the very *being* of the subject. The situation is, to be sure, contradictory. In being posited as Other the subject experiences itself as being, *in its very being*, an object. This is different to the way in which every subject sees itself epistemologically as an object in the everyday structure of self-reflection or self-knowledge. Precisely because it is an existential transformation, to be posited as Other involves, for Beauvoir, a limitation of the freedom of the subject, something which Sartre believed to be impossible. It is interesting that the degraded condition of the Other described in *The Second Sex* is precisely the condition that, in Beauvoir's earlier work called forth, in rage and hate, the desire, even need, for vengeance. It was left to Valerie Solanas, in her 1967 S.C.U.M. Manifesto[14], to make this connection explicit.

By introducing the concept of the Other, *The Second Sex* provides an initial answer to the question 'what is a woman?' She is the Other. As an existential answer to an existential question this makes an historical claim about woman's situation and involves no commitment to the idea of an essential nature. The justification for the claim lies in the next 650 pages of *The Second Sex*. In often excruciating detail, Beauvoir heaps example upon example in a sustained trawl through the evidence for the secondary status of women in European history, their eradication as subjects in law, their status as possession or chattel, their special exploitation in the labour force, and so on. She documents the casual misogyny and contempt for women, the ridiculous but pernicious myths and fantasies of 'femininity' and 'womanhood' that litter the pages of (mainly French) male-authored literature. She recounts the gradual but decisive suppression of the vitality, ambition and freedom of little girls being taught to be young women; the mutilation of all adolescent and adult (male and female) sexuality in the dominant view of heterosexual relations as 'possession' of the female; the institutionalized renunciation of female agency and desire in the cul-de-sac of the 'destiny' of marriage; the impossibility of motherhood as a freely chosen project under current conditions; the social horror of the ageing and old woman; and the stereotypical feminine character types to which, in desperation, this oppression gives rise. It was French women's nascent opposition to all of this and their growing demands for certain basic rights (the right to vote, the right to use contraception) that had provoked the masculine anxiety about 'that mysterious threatened reality called "femininity"' which Beauvoir ridiculed in *The Second Sex*.

However, as an historical claim the idea that woman is Other immediately leads today's readers to question its contemporary relevance. In a section on 'The Independent Woman' Beauvoir herself looked forward to a different future, her own life functioning, to some extent, as the model for liberated womanhood. Thanks in part to *The Second Sex*, has that future not arrived, in Western Europe at least? Do we still need a feminist politics or are we, as some theorists and journalists now like to claim, living in a 'post-feminist' world?

Certainly the generality of the claim that 'woman is other' needs finessing. But the idea that several thousands of years of history could be overturned by a couple of decades of concerted feminism is childish, to say the least. It is also blind to some basic facts, hoodwinked by the achievement of certain formal equalities (the right to vote and so on) and intoxicated by certain novel social (specifically sexual and behavioural) liberties. Why does the responsibility for child and other care fall disproportionately to women, such that it is experienced as a burden? Why are women still paid less for doing the same work as men? Why is male on female rape still so prevalent, taking new, chemically facilitated forms? Why are little girls still encouraged to dream of marrying a prince? Why are puerile, sexist magazines so popular among men? Why do women consent to appear in them? Why do women's magazines presume that heterosexual partnering is the first priority for all women? Why do so many girls and women hate and harm their healthy bodies? Why is ageing still seen as such a catastrophe for so many women? Until we no longer need to ask these questions, we would be well advised not to presume that Beauvoir does not have anything relevant to say about men and women's existences today.

7

SEX

[B]iological considerations are extremely important. In the history of woman they play a part of the first rank and constitute an essential element in her situation. Throughout our further discussion we shall always bear them in mind ... But I deny that they establish for her a fixed and inevitable destiny. They are insufficient for setting up a hierarchy of the sexes; they fail to explain why woman is the Other; they do not condemn her to remain in this subordinate role for ever.

It has frequently been maintained that in physiology alone must be sought the answers to these questions: Are the chances for individual success the same in the two sexes? Which plays the more important role in the species? But it must be noted that the first of these problems is quite different in the case of woman as compared with other females; for animal species are fixed and it is possible to define them in static terms ... whereas the human species is for ever in a state of becoming ...

It is only in a human perspective that we can compare the male and the female of the human species. But man is defined as a being who is not fixed, who makes himself what he is. As Merleau-Ponty very justly puts it, man is not a natural species: he is a historical idea. Woman is not a completed reality, but rather a becoming, and it is in her becoming that she should be compared with man; that is to say, her possibilities should be defined . . .

Thus we must view the facts of biology in the light of an ontological, economic, social, and psychological context. The enslavement of the female to the species and the limitations of her various powers are extremely important facts; the body of woman is one of the essential elements in her situation in the world. But that body is not enough to define her as woman; there is no true living reality except as manifested by the conscious individual through activities and in the bosom of a society. Biology is not enough to give an answer to the question that is before us: why is woman the *Other*? Our task is to discover how nature . . . has been affected throughout the course of history; we are concerned to find out what humanity has made of the human female.

The Second Sex, pp.65–66 and 69.

One is not born, but rather becomes, a woman. No biological, psychological or economic fate determines the figure that the human female presents in society; it is civilization as a whole that produces this creature, intermediate between male and eunuch, which is described as feminine.

The Second Sex, p.295.

Having claimed, in the Introduction to *The Second Sex*, that 'woman is Other', one of Beauvoir's chief tasks in the rest of the book was to answer the question: why? *Why* is woman Other? What accounts for the fact that women occupy the position and suffer under the limitations that they do? The first part of *The Second Sex*, ironically entitled 'Destiny', consists of three chapters, each of which is devoted to different kinds of explanation for woman's position as Other: the biological, the psychoanalytic and the economic (broadly, Marxian), respectively.

The first of these is the most interesting, because it is the most philosophically astute and the most challenging, even though the object of its attack is the most crude. It contains the theoretical justification for, and explanation of, the most famous line in all of Beauvoir's published work: 'One is not born, but rather becomes, a woman.' As a philosophical rebuttal of reductive biological explanations for women's social subordination it is particularly important today. In the context of the popularity (but rarely the understanding) of physiological and genetic explanations for almost everything – criminality, alcoholism, rape, patriarchy, economic success, and so on – it offers us a model for approaching these claims critically. It does this simply, but powerfully, by insisting on the need for reflection on the basic terms and presumptions of these claims for biology's explanatory power, which are also the basic terms of our everyday presumptions about sex. In these extracts, the reader is doubly interpellated – critically, as bearers of these presumptions, and existentially, as bearers of sex.

Beauvoir shows that physio-biological explanations for women's historical subordination to men rest upon the meaning ascribed to sex difference. The definition of 'sex' concerns only the different roles of each of its two terms – male and female – in reproduction. Thus we are able to speak generally of females and males across species, and identify some common elements in otherwise distinctly different animals – between humans and mice, for example, to the extent that both bear live young. In physio-biological explanations of women's subordination (which also function as justifications for it), these common elements are thought to outweigh all species differences. They are thus based on the presumption of an ontological equivalence between the human and the animal, that is, a presumption that the *being* of the human is equivalent to the *being* of the animal, or even the *being* of the insect. We can see this in contemporary evolutionary biology and psychology. In one recent and well-publicized evolutionary-psychological thesis, for example, the existence of a certain grasping organ on the abdomens of male scorpionflies, which the authors call a 'rape appendage', is the basis for the extrapolated claim that the human male has developed with an innate 'mental' tendency to rape. In this justificatory biological explanation for male on female rape, the continuum from fly to man is uninterrupted – they inhabit the same plane of being.

Beauvoir's main point in these extracts is to assert, against the presumption of sameness, the fundamental difference between human existence and animal life. Although Beauvoir reserves the word 'animal' to refer to non-human species, human being is, of course, *also* animal being. The distinction between human existence and animal life is marked in the distinctions between the existential categories of woman and man on the one hand, and the biological categories of the human female and male on the other. Beauvoir's claim that 'animal species are fixed and it is possible to define them in static terms . . . whereas the human species is for ever in a state of becoming' does not assert that animal species, unlike the human, do not evolve. It claims that at any given moment it is possible to describe animal species statically – to say, for example, that the mare does or does not run as fast as the stallion – and that this objective and fixed state of affairs may be the basis for explanations of other aspects of the species' social organizations. On the other hand, although we may be able to proffer similar kinds of descriptions for humans – for example, the human female is generally smaller than the male – such facts (if such they are) need to be seen *within* the whole context of human existence and therefore cannot form the objective basis for an explanation *of* existence. Humanity is, Beauvoir says, free 'transcendence and surpassing'. That is, human existence is distinctive in its constant movement beyond the given, its capacity for transforming the given. To the extent that its own animal being is one of its givens, human existence is ontologically distinctive in its capacity to transcend and surpass aspects of its own being.

According to Beauvoir, sex difference is one of the facts or givens of biology: it defines the distinction between the human female and the male in their animal being. The question is, then, in what sense, and to what extent, can the fact or given of sex be transcended or surpassed by women and men? Relating this to the specific question of women's subordination, Beauvoir's argument looks at first decidedly double-edged. It is pursued in a discussion of what she calls 'the enslavement of the female to the species'. This discussion, and its relation to the later chapter on 'The Mother', has attracted much criticism from feminists, and it is not difficult to see why. According to Beauvoir, the 'female organism is wholly adapted for and subservient to maternity' (*The Second Sex*, p.52), such that her individual life is subordinated to the function of the reproduction of the species through her, 'absorbing' her individual life. This means that 'the individuality of the female is opposed by the interest of the species' and the most highly developed female – the human – feels this 'enslavement' most keenly. (*The Second Sex*, p.56) This sounds grim, but Beauvoir's pessimism is partly rhetorical. The burden of the human female is accentuated in order that the rather different plight of the *woman* might emerge more clearly. For 'the burden imposed on woman by her reproductive function' is not naturally, but *socially*, determined.

> The bondage of woman to the species is more or less rigorous according to the number of births demanded by society and the degree of hygienic care provided for pregnancy and childbirth. Thus, while it is true that in the higher *animals* the individual existence is asserted more imperiously by the male than by the female, *in the human species* individual 'possibilities' depend upon the economic and social situation. (*The Second Sex*, p.67, emphasis added.)

Given the right social and economic situation, woman's role in reproduction – the biological given of her being female – would not necessarily conflict with her individuality at all.

To this extent, sex can indeed be 'surpassed' or 'overcome', according to Beauvoir. This is not to say that it can be left behind –

this is not the meaning of the existentialist concepts of surpassing and overcoming. The facts of biology, Beauvoir says, cannot
be denied, and she repeatedly emphasizes their importance. The
bulk of the chapter on biological explanation is a mass of detail
on, for example, the physiology of menstruation and reproduction, with no suggestion that these physiological givens can be
avoided. (Perhaps this explains the otherwise strange fact that it
was a specialist in biological aspects of sex, H. M. Parshley, who
was approached by an American publisher to assess Beauvoir's
book as a likely candidate for translation, and who subsequently
loosely translated an abridged version for readers of English.) The
facts of biology cannot be denied, but 'in themselves they have no
significance' (*The Second Sex*, p.66). This is to say that the significance that they are allowed to have for human existence is
bestowed upon them, not *derived from* them. In itself, the fact of sex
difference cannot determine the form of social existence of men
and women; in itself, it cannot account for the historical fact that
woman is Other. On the contrary the social existence of men and
women determines how sex difference will be lived and what
it will mean, and in the social context in which woman is Other
sex is, according to Beauvoir, lived by the woman as a burden
or (as she hyperbolically puts it) 'enslavement'. Beauvoir's conclusion is that as it is woman, not the human female, who is Other,
her position must be explained in existential, not biological,
terms.

The most general point here concerns what we might legiti-
mately say about the explanatory power of any fact of biology,
given the distinctive character of human existence. However, it
is the alleged explanatory power of sex difference that most often
concerns us today. What difference does sex difference make?
How much of the social and cultural difference between boys
and girls and men and women can be explained by the biological and physio-chemical aspects of our sex? These are questions
on which everyone seems to have an opinion, and in relation to
which the Sunday-supplement culture of popular science is

always pleased to find the latest evidence apparently confirming what we already knew: boys will be boys. Of course, if we are sure that boys will be boys and girls will be girls we are relieved of the burden of thinking about things further. But this is another example of that 'bad faith' which Beauvoir identified in the '*que sera sera*' of American racism. It rests on the presumption that animal life trumps human existence and absolves itself of the burden of responsibility for the form of the latter. Beauvoir, on the other hand, insisted on the priority of human existence over animal life. In *The Second Sex*, this amounts to the priority of the category of the woman over that of the female.

In the great 'second wave' of Anglophone feminist theory and activism, beginning in the 1960s, Beauvoir's distinction between the female and the woman was understood in terms of a distinction between sex and gender. According to this distinction, 'sex' refers to biology, whereas 'gender' refers to society or culture. Although sex may be fixed, gender – understood as the different sets of socio-culturally determined behavioural characteristics of, and expectations for, men and women – is not. In pointing out that much that was previously imagined to be the effect of sex was in fact the social expression of gender, feminists gained the theoretical lever to argue for the possibility of change. The analysis and criticism of the norms of gender then became – and to a very great extent still are – the basis of modern feminism. Retrospectively, this emphasis on gender can be identified in the feminist tracts and politics of the nineteenth century, even if the terminology of sex and gender was not then current.

In fact, strictly speaking, Beauvoir's distinction between the female and the woman does not map directly onto the categories of sex and gender. Beauvoir's 'woman' is an existential category that cuts across the distinction between nature and culture on which the sex/gender distinction implicitly depends.[15] Even so, the political effects of identifying Beauvoir's categories with the Anglophone sex/gender distinction were considerable, and not opposed to Beauvoir's intentions. It would be churlish to pick at it now were it not for the fact that it blinds us to one of the most radical implications of this section of *The Second Sex*, an implication of which Beauvoir herself was probably not aware. The sex/gender distinction leaves the domain of sex itself unquestioned and unchallenged, whereas Beauvoir's existentialist analysis of the relation between the female and the woman does not.

The challenge is contained within Beauvoir's claim that, although the givens of biology cannot be denied, 'in themselves they have no significance'. This means, among other things, that our knowledge of the physiology and anatomy of human bodies – including the basic distinctions between their parts – is, like all the facts of biology, dependent on a *context* of knowledge that constitutes its objects of study as objects. In the development of areas of knowledge, scientists and others define what it is they are studying, rather than coming across already pre-defined categories of things. Although this is guaranteed to send some readers into paroxysms of indignation on behalf of 'common sense', properly understood it need not. In relation to relatively uncontentious examples we can see that this does not destroy the possibility of scientific knowledge, but, rather, makes it possible. For example, neuroscientists have identified a discrete object of knowledge called the 'corpus callosum', a part of the brain that consists of a bundle of fibres that connects the right and left hemispheres. However, the fibres of the corpus callosum connect to and are entangled with the other parts of the brain, such that it is difficult to separate them. Where do the connecting fibres of the corpus callosum, which reach out into the cerebrum, cease to be part of former and become part of the latter? The impossibility of answering this question shows that this, like other named parts of the brain, is a relatively arbitrary subdivision that we treat, for the purposes of scientific research, as discrete biological entities.[16]

In the same way, but more contentiously, Beauvoir's argument implies that the division of the human animal into the two discrete and mutually exclusive categories of male and female – the presumption of binary sex difference itself – is the imposition of a certain meaning on a set of otherwise inherently meaningless physiological differences. As Beauvoir points out – not denying, but paying close attention to 'the facts of biology' – the embryonic tissues from which the ovaries and testes develop is at first undifferentiated, which accounts for the many intermediate states between hermaphroditism and gonochorism (sexual separation): 'Even in those species exhibiting a high degree of sexual differentiation individuals combining both male and female characteristics may occur. Many cases of intersexuality are known in both animals and man.' (*The Second Sex*, p.47) According to some estimates, around 1.7 per cent of all human births are intersex infants, that is, infants who are not easily classifiable as either male or female.[17] Where the medical establishment notices them, these infants are subject to unnecessary (that is, not life saving) surgery and chemical 'management' in the attempt to make them *look*, even if they cannot be made to *be*, 'properly' male or female – a process which usually continues for many years, sometimes even a lifetime of chemical management.

What determines that these infants be treated as anomalous and abnormal, rather than examples of the tremendous diversity of human morphology? Not the facts of biology themselves, as Beauvoir shows, but our determination to interpret them according to the presumption of binary sex difference. This is particularly clear where the child's genital ambiguity is such that physicians are forced to ask themselves: when is a penis really a clitoris? Or when is a clitoris really a penis? The decision can only be made according to a crude measurement on an arbitrarily determined scale in which the neonate organ between 1 and 2.5 centimetres in length is medically acceptable as neither clitoris nor penis. The treatment of intersex infants is a process of attempted normalization according to the social expectation that we must all be either male or female – something the medical practitioners involved do not deny – whilst simultaneously acknowledging that we all are not. The radical philosophical and political challenge of *The Second Sex* is to think beyond the social expectation of sex difference. Are we any more prepared for this in the twenty-first century than Beauvoir's contemporaries were in 1949?

8

SEXUALITY

'Oh! You're already in bed!' said Brogan. His arms laden with spotlessly clean washing, he looked at me, questioningly. 'I wanted to change the sheets.'

'It's not necessary.' He remained in the doorway, embarrassed by his magnificent burden. 'I'm quite happy like this', I said, pulling the warm sheet in which he had slept the night before up to my chin. He moved away; he came back.

'Anne!'

He had thrown himself on me, and his voice shook me through and through. For the first time I spoke his name: 'Lewis!'

'Anne! I'm so happy!'

He was naked, I was naked, and yet I felt not the slightest embarrassment; his gaze could not hurt me; he did not judge me, he would not put anything before me. From my head to my toes his hands were learning me by heart. Again I said: 'I love your hands.'

'You love them?'

'All evening I've been wondering if I would feel them on my body.'

'You will – all night', he said.

Suddenly he was no longer either awkward or modest. His desire transfigured me. I, who had been for so long without taste, without form, once again had breasts, belly, sex, flesh; I was as nourishing as bread, as fragrant as the earth. It was so miraculous that I did not think to measure the time or my pleasure; I only know that the faint chirping of dawn could be heard as we fell asleep. [. . .]

Les mandarins (*The Mandarins*), pp.38–9.

Beauvoir's novels usually comprise a complex combination of literary, philosophical and autobiographical elements. This often got her into trouble. Her first two novels, *She Came to Stay* (1943) and *The Blood of Others* (1945) were both well received, but they attracted the criticism of didacticism. Both present philosophical problems in literary form. The internal monologues and the dialogue of their characters are often expressions of the anxiety provoked by certain philosophical realizations or even take the form of impromptu, informal philosophical debate. They are, to some extent, existentialist showcases. The charge against them was that their status as literature was compromised by their being merely vehicles for ideas. In a 1945 lecture, subsequently published as 'Literature and Metaphysics' (1946), Beauvoir replied to this criticism in a defence of the 'metaphysical novel'. It is true, Beauvoir says, that the novel is only justified to the extent that 'it is a mode of communication irreducible to any other'. ('Literature and Metaphysics', p.270) A novel that merely drapes a previously constructed philosophy in the 'shimmering garment' ('Literature and Metaphysics', p.272) of fiction is unjustifiable as a novel. But there can be no absolute distinction between literature and philosophy because they are both only different forms of 'an original grasping of metaphysical reality' or different ways of making it explicit. ('Literature and Metaphysics', p.273)

What is 'metaphysical reality'? For Beauvoir, it is the truth of human existence in the world. It is 'metaphysical' to the extent that it goes beyond the individual and the individual's capacity to encompass its totality in thought, whilst still being the truth revealed *by* and *for* the individual. One does not grasp this truth by studying metaphysics. Metaphysics, Beauvoir says, is not something that one *does*, like mathematics or physics; one *is* metaphysical. Metaphysics is an 'attitude'. The child, adopting this attitude by default, 'concretely discovers its presence in the world, its abandonment, its freedom, the opacity of things, and the resistance of foreign consciousnesses'. Although there is no one to whom an aspect of metaphysical reality has not been revealed at some point in their life – because 'every human event possesses a metaphysical signification' ('Literature and Metaphysics', p.273) – it is the special task of philosophers and novelists to reveal it to us.

The difference between philosophy and literature is the *way* in which each does this. Philosophy, according to Beauvoir, uses abstract language in the development of theories in which metaphysical experience is 'more or less systematized in its essential character, thus as timeless and objective'. ('Literature and Metaphysics', p.273) Literature, on the other hand, expresses the universal meaning of metaphysical experience in its 'subjective, singular, and dramatic character . . . as it is disclosed in the living relation that is action and feeling'. ('Literature and Metaphysics', p.275) However, philosophy and literature are at their best when each contains elements characteristic of the other. For Beauvoir, existentialist philosophy is best able to describe the universal aspects of existence precisely because it underscores the 'role and value of subjectivity' ('Literature and Metaphysics', p.274) and retains an emphasis on the concrete aspects of lived experience. In the same way, the novel in which the metaphysical attitude is made explicit is the novel *par excellence*. In fact 'Literature and Metaphysics' ends with the claim that the metaphysical novel 'provides a disclosure of existence unequalled by any other mode of expression' ('Literature and Metaphysics', p.276), seemingly announcing what amounts to, in her view, the priority of this form of literature over philosophy.

In Beauvoir's own novels, the relationship between literature and philosophy is often mediated by a third term: autobiography. This is nowhere more obvious than in *The Mandarins* (1954), the novel from which this chapter's extract is taken. The novel is set in the 'changed world' to which Beauvoir says she awoke in 1945, at the end of the war. It describes the dashing of the hopes of the intellectual Left and the messy political compromises that they were forced – but also allowed themselves – to make. It tackles, among other things, the problem of knowing what do with the former collaborators of the Vichy regime, the acute problem that the Stalinism of Soviet communism posed for the French Left, and the looming shadow of American imperialism in Europe. As Beauvoir wrote in her reflections on the novel in her autobiography, *The Mandarins* is about '*us*', the intellectuals in Beauvoir's circles at that time. (*Force of Circumstance*, p.276–7) Through the first person voice of one of its two main characters, Anne Dubreuilh, it is also about a passionate and painful trans-atlantic love affair between a female Parisian intellectual and her male lover, a writer from Chicago. (Anne is the 'I' in the extract above.) It is, as Beauvoir wrote more than once to Nelson Algren '*our* story . . . a nowadays kind of story, this love from Paris to Chicago, with airplanes making the towns so near, yet so far'. (*Beloved Chicago Man*, p.421)

The extent of the autobiographical basis of the details of Anne and Lewis's story is clear from Beauvoir's autobiography, her let-ters to Algren and the relevant sections of *America Day by Day*. Beauvoir's willingness to expose her life – albeit often novelisti-cally transfigured – was in part based on her belief that one's life was, in fact, a public entity. This does not mean that she thought privacy was not desirable or even necessary, or that a domestic space of one's own was not a requirement for a liveable life. It is a claim about the sort of thing a life is, based on a certain philo-sophical view of the sort of thing a 'self' is. In *The Transcendence of the Ego* (1936), Sartre argued, following the German philoso-pher Edmund Husserl, that 'the existence of consciousness is absolute [i.e. indubitable] because consciousness is conscious of itself' and it cannot be mistaken about this. But 'consciousness is purely and simply consciousness of being consciousness of [an] object'. This means that consciousness is not itself its own object: one cannot be solely conscious of consciousness without any content, for consciousness is always consciousness *of* something. Further, there is no 'ego' 'inhabiting' consciousness – no thing, substance or even unifying principle *within* consciousness that we could identify as the bearer of or condition for consciousness's consciousness of objects. For Sartre, the ego is a 'transcendent object', by which he means that the unity of what I call 'I' is found not 'inside' me but in 'the unity of states and of actions' that are directly observable and 'outside' me.[18]

In 1960, in the second volume of her autobiography, Beauvoir wrote: 'I still believe to this day in the theory of the "transcendental ego".[19] The self has only a probable objectivity, and anyone saying "I" only grasps the outer edge of it; an outsider can get a clearer and more accurate picture . . . Self-knowledge is impossible, and the best one can hope for is self-revelation.' (*The Prime of Life*, p.368) Accordingly, Beauvoir did not conceive of the four volumes of her autobiography as a confession. It was not the exposure of the intimate truth of her own existence, a truth to which she had privileged access. It was a way of recounting events, presenting them as objective realities, in order to 'assume' these events, or make sense of them, to see who she herself was from the outside. This is particularly clear in the frequent episodes of self-criticism. Retrospectively, seeing her past self objectively, she is able to see certain truths about herself that were, at the time, invisible.

In her novels the autobiographical elements take on a similarly objective form, but to a somewhat different end. They provide the 'subjective, singular aspect of experience' through which, according to Beauvoir, literature reveals the universal aspects of 'metaphysical reality'. This allows us to understand why Beauvoir insisted, despite the obvious modelling of Anne and Lewis's relationship on her affair with Algren, that it was not a roman-à-cléf.

The extent and the manner of fiction's dependence on real life is of small importance; the fiction is built only by pulverizing all these sources and then allowing a new existence to be reborn from them. The gossips who poke about among the ashes let the work that is offered them escape, and the shards they rout out are worth nothing; no fact has any truth unless it is placed in its true context. (*Force of Circumstance*, p.279)

That is, we miss the point of *The Mandarins* if we read it only for what it reveals about Beauvoir's life (or others' lives). Furthermore, anything that it might reveal in this respect is unreliable because it lacks its concrete context. The 'subjective' element of literature – even when it is clearly autobiographical – is important only to the extent that it reveals universal aspects of existence. To some extent, this must also be true of autobiography itself. This allows us to approach one of the abiding themes of Beauvoir's work – sexuality – without prurience. According to the terms of 'Literature and Metaphysics', the subjective, singular aspect of *sexual* experience would have a peculiar 'metaphysical signification', its description revealing an aspect of 'metaphysical reality'. Beauvoir leaves it up to us to work out what this is.

In *The Mandarins* the character of Anne gives us a clue. From the beginning her sexual being is an issue. The first social event in the novel – a post-war Christmas party – is replayed from different perspectives, the second time through Anne's eyes. In one of the first examples of Beauvoir's cinematic style in *The Mandarins* we jump backwards and forwards between Anne's melancholy, hung-over post-party thoughts and the scene of the party itself. In the midst of the party Anne's thoughts shift from her daughter and her various friends to herself:

I walked over to the buffet and poured myself a brandy. My eyes glanced down along my black skirt and stopped at my legs. It was funny to think I had legs; no one ever noticed them, not even myself. They were slender and well-shaped in their beige stockings,

certainly no less well-shaped than many another pair. And yet one
day they'd be buried in the earth without ever having existed. It
seemed unfair. (*The Mandarins*, p.37)

Anne's reverie is interrupted by Scriassine, who had 'fled
Austria after having fled Russia' and had immediately taken an
interest in Anne's celebrated writer husband and his young political friends on his arrival in Paris but who 'never seemed to
notice that I existed'. (*The Mandarins*, p.38) Anne realises he is
trying to seduce her and some ten pages later, when he asks her
out for dinner she decides to accept: 'Well, well! At least for him
I have legs!' (*The Mandarins*, p.44) During that dinner Scriassine
asks Anne how often she has taken advantage of the (sexual) freedom on which her marriage is based. 'Occasionally', she tells
him, whilst reflecting to herself that she has in fact lived in
chastity for five years and believed she would do so forever: 'It
seemed natural to me for my life as a woman to be ended; there
were so many things that had ended, forever . . .' (*The Mandarins*,
p.86) Their ensuing sexual encounter is described as an almost
violent reawakening of desire, the bursting into bloom of a
'mutilated' flower. (The sexual detail is completely omitted in
the English translation.)

After her second meeting with Scriassine it is clear that there
will be no further sexual relations between them. Having 'found
herself' again after five years of chastity, Anne once again feels
herself condemned to sexlessness. (*The Mandarins*, p.93)
Although her subsequent love affair with Lewis is sexually, emo-
tionally and intellectually more significant and satisfying, its end
leaves her in the same position, facing a future without sexual
love. The first and the last we hear from Anne in *The Mandarins*
are her thoughts on her own death. Although these encompass
the inevitability of actual death and the possibility of suicide,
their intertwining with the theme of sexuality complicates their
meaning. The now-traditional literary and philosophical treatment of the relation between sex and death trades on the

biological relation between the function of the former and the fact of the latter, giving sex its charge and pseudo-gothic horror. To the extent that, as Beauvoir pointed out in the Introduction to *The Second Sex*, woman stands in for sex, the sex-death theme often appears in misogynistic or gynophobic forms. In *The Mandarins* the opposite is the case. Sexlessness, not sex, is 'death'. Existence is mutilated by sexual death.

From this we could extrapolate the possible 'metaphysical signification' of the experience of sexuality in *The Mandarins*. Although it leans on its physiological basis, sexuality is an existential phenomenon. In Beauvoir's terms, though animals may have sex they do not have sexuality. It may be that, for Beauvoir, as a particular mode of embodied existence, sexuality reveals the 'metaphysical reality' of the fundamental ambiguity of human existence, but with a different slant to its presentation in her earlier work. For the possibility that may be realized in sexuality, as we see in Anne, is that of the facticity of the body lived in *pleasure*. The free 'assumption' of the facticity of the sexed body transcends the sexual function of reproduction which cannot therefore define or explain sexuality. Metaphysically (if not socially), sexuality is neither hetero- nor homosexuality, nor necessarily any combination of both. To this extent Beauvoir's description of sexual existence is part of the more general vitalist exuberance that runs like a subterranean stream through her work, surfacing where it has its opportunities.

However, one needs to move beyond the limits of the terms of 'Literature and Metaphysics' to see the full importance of the theme of sexuality in Beauvoir's work. For it is politics, not metaphysics, that is really at issue. From early on female sexuality is presented in Beauvoir's work with an astonishing frankness. Here the phrase 'female sexuality' does not refer to any specifically female form of desire or pleasure. It refers simply to the fact that girls and women are sexual beings who experience and act on their sexual desires. In mid-century Europe it was still quite something to admit this openly. In the first volume of her autobiography Beauvoir describes her twelve-year-old self 'prey to agonized desires, with parched mouth', tossing and turning in bed 'calling for a man's body to be pressed against my own, for a man's hand to stroke my flesh'. (*Memoirs of a Dutiful Daughter*, p.100) Later, recalling her early twenties, Beauvoir speaks of the 'actual *pain*' of unfulfilled sexual desire when she is parted from Sartre:

> I was forced to admit a truth that I had been doing my best to conceal ever since adolescence: my physical desires were greater than I wanted them to be . . . In the night train from Tours to Paris the touch of an anonymous hand along my leg could arouse feelings – against my conscious will – of quite shattering intensity. (*The Prime of Life*, p.63)

In an interview in 1976, asked what she would change if she rewrote her autobiography, Beauvoir's answer was quick:

> I would give a very frank account of my sexuality. Yes, a truly sincere account, and from a feminist point of view. Today, I would like to tell women how I lived my sexuality because it is a political, not individual, issue. At the time I didn't do it because I hadn't understood the magnitude and importance of this issue, nor the necessity for individual honesty.[20]

Beauvoir is probably referring here to her sexual relationships with women, of which there is not a word in her autobiography. In relation to all aspects of female sexuality, however, the political point is the same. The actuality and expression of female desire is nothing like the 'official' version promulgated by the 'myths of femininity' that Beauvoir exposed in *The Second Sex*.

In light of this, Anne's story in *The Mandarins* takes on a different hue. The affair with Lewis is not, as some critics suggested, a romantic interlude in an otherwise political novel, it is part of the political theme of female sexuality. Anne's five years of chastity were not matched by her husband Robert, to whom 'it seemed normal to pick up a pretty whore in a bar and to spend an hour with her.' (*Les mandarins*, pp.117–18) For Anne the tragedy of the end of her sexual existence is always bound up with her age. She is haunted by the idea that sexuality is inappropriate for a woman after forty, whereas her husband, who is significantly older, has no such qualms. In the end, however, the political and the metaphysical intertwine in the presentation of Anne's sexuality. Anne's 'sexual death' is socially, not biologically, determined. It is not the end of desire, but – what is existentially much worse – the *repression* of desire. It was, according to Beauvoir, up to another figure entirely – the Marquis de Sade – to show us a way out of this trap.

9

PERVERSION

Sade's enthusiasts have hailed him as a prophetic genius; they claim that his work heralds Nietzsche, Stirner, Freud and surrealism. But this cult, founded, like all cults, on a misconception, by deifying the 'divine marquis' only betrays him. The critics who make of Sade neither villain nor idol, but a man and a writer, can be counted upon the fingers of one hand. Thanks to them, Sade has come back at last to earth, among us.

Just what is his place, however? Why does he merit our interest? Even his admirers will readily admit that his work is, for the most part, unreadable; philosophically, it escapes banality only to founder in incoherence. As to his vices, they are not startlingly original; Sade invented nothing in this domain, and one finds in psychiatric treatises a profusion of cases at least as interesting as his. The fact is that it is neither as author nor as sexual pervert that Sade compels our attention; it is by virtue of the relationship which he created between these two aspects of himself. Sade's aberrations begin to acquire value when, instead of enduring them as his fixed nature, he elaborates an immense system in order to justify them. Inversely, his books take hold of us as soon as we become aware that for all their repetitiousness, their platitudes and clumsiness, he is trying to communicate an experience whose distinguishing characteristic is, nevertheless, a tendency to be incommunicable. Sade tried to make of his psycho-physical destiny an ethical choice; and of this act, in which he assumed his 'separateness', he attempted to make an example and an appeal. It is thus that his adventure assumes a wide human significance. Can we, without renouncing our individuality, satisfy our aspirations to universality? Or is it only by the sacrifice of our individual differences that we can integrate ourselves into the community? This problem concerns us all. In Sade the differences are carried to the point of outrageousness, and the immensity of his literary effort shows how passionately he wished to be accepted by the human community. Thus, we find in his work the most extreme form of the conflict from which no individual can escape without self-deception. It is the paradox and, in a sense, the triumph of Sade that his persistent singularity helps us to define the human drama in its general aspect.

'Must We Burn Sade?' pp.4–5.

Simone de Beauvoir and the Marquis de Sade shared more than the aristocratic form of their names. They were both decried as pornographers (with some justification for the title in Sade's case) and both had reputations as notorious sexual libertines. If Sade cultivated this reputation, it accrued to Beauvoir by virtue of her being a woman, since a man who behaved like Beauvoir (rejecting monogamy, enjoying sex outside marriage, and so on) was nothing remarkable. As Sade occupied a special place in twentieth-century French intellectual life, it was not surprising that he should come under Beauvoir's gaze. Like most – if not all – of her peers Beauvoir had read some of Sade's works but found them 'ridiculous . . . boring . . . too abstract and schematic'. However, around 1948, reading Sade's *Justine* was a 'revelation'. Beauvoir had been asked to write a preface for a new edition of *Justine* but declined, citing the need to 'study the subject' more. Her interest piqued, she went, once again, to the Bibliothèque nationale to read. At that time one read authors like Sade in 'Hell' (*L'Enfer*), as the room in the library for consulting the collection of proscribed books (*L'Enfermé*) was called for short. (*Force of Circumstance*, p.255) Beauvoir, it is clear, relished the whole episode. Her ensuing psycho-philosophical analysis of Sade's erotic 'system' is not uncritical, but it is largely positive. It is thus tempting to speculate on the nature of Beauvoir's identification with Sade. What is the basis of Beauvoir's sympathy for this devil?

Beauvoir begins her essay with a conventional claim – Sade's works are neither erotically stimulating, philosophically original or aesthetically well achieved. Why, then, 'does he merit our interest?' In one sense the answer is obvious. Sade was a stupendous pervert, and perverts and their perversions exercise an enduring attraction over us all. But Beauvoir's question is asked in the context of the complaint that Sade is 'scandalously' absent in standard histories of eighteenth-century ideas, with the implication that his entitlement to a place there must be justified. Beauvoir's essay explicitly sets out to legitimate Sade's 'place in French literature', which 'he is still a long way from having won . . . officially'. ('Must We Burn Sade?', p.4) Thus it will not be our pleasantly scandalized interest in Sade's perversions *per se* (Sade eats shit!), but what he makes of his perversions in the adventure of his existence and the universal significance of his efforts that will claim our interest. More specifically, it is in laying bare 'the supreme value of his testimony' ('Must We Burn Sade?', p.64) that he will be shown to *merit* our interest. From the beginning, then, it is not just Sade who needs justifying, but also our interest in him.

Although, according to Beauvoir, no one would think of ranking *Justine* with *Manon Lescaut* or *Les liaisons dangereuses* ('Must We Burn Sade?', p.37), Beauvoir treated Sade, Abbé Prevost and Laclos equally as authors, expecting (and finding) in his work that same revelation of 'metaphysical reality' described as the task of literature in 'Literature and Metaphysics'. As in many of Beauvoir's essays, the theses announced at the beginning of 'Must We Burn Sade?' grow and are transformed throughout the essay. But in its first presentation, as this extract shows, Beauvoir's argument centres on two main claims. First, in 'assuming' his 'aberrations', rather than enduring them as a natural imposition, Sade made his 'psycho-physical destiny' an ethical choice. This choice is ethical because he transcends the mere fact of his psycho-physical make-up by conferring an absolute value upon the aberrations that constituted it. In an extreme form, Sade demonstrates a general truth: the subjective origin of all value. If nothing has a value in itself, but only that which we confer on it, then anything can be valued, as the case of Sade shows. He also, unusually, demonstrates what is otherwise only implicit in Beauvoir's (and Sartre's) existentialist account of the subjective origin of value: the possibility of a singular ethic, a one-man morality. Further, he represents what, for most people, is the problem with such a possibility: Sade is a monster whose personal 'ethic' abuses others.

In 'Must We Burn Sade?' Beauvoir is clear that Sade's ethic is not one to be emulated: 'every time we side with a child whose throat has been slit by a sex maniac, we take a stand against him.' ('Must We Burn Sade?', p.61) Nevertheless his life has, she says, 'an exemplary character' to the extent that the form (rather than content) of his ethic and its metaphysical motivation has a universal significance. This is explained in the elaboration of the second main claim from the opening pages of Beauvoir's essay and concerns Sade's commitment to the principle of subjectivity. Sade's merit lies 'in his having proclaimed aloud what everyone admits with shame to himself' ('Must We Burn Sade?', p.63): the irrecusable fact of the 'separateness' of each individual. This fact is dramatized in Sade's 'persistent singularity': 'he had no fellow but himself'. ('Must We Burn Sade?', p.18) For Sade this singularity was so extreme as to be pathological. His insistent intensification of his 'separateness' produced an autistic ethic that benefited no one. The salient feature of Sade's 'tormented life' was, according to Beauvoir, 'that the painful experience of living never revealed to him any solidarity between other men and himself'. ('Must We Burn Sade?', p.18)

But without following Sade's pathology we can, according to
Beauvoir, thank him for revealing the condition of possibility
for any ethic that goes beyond him: 'If we ever hope to transcend the separateness of individuals, we may do so only on
condition that we be aware of its existence. Otherwise, promises
of happiness and justice conceal the worst dangers.' ('Must We
Burn Sade?', p.63)

This point about Sade's exemplarity in the assumption of separateness remains abstract in its first presentation but is developed
in Beauvoir's subsequent justification of Sade. As well as making
his sexuality an ethic, Sade deserved, according to Beauvoir, 'to
be hailed as a great moralist'. ('Must We Burn Sade?', p.40) His
ethic and his morality are two different things. The former was
Sade's baroque elaboration of his own sexual pleasure into a
principle that excluded all others from consideration. It was born
from what Beauvoir identifies as the flash of insight that illumi-
nates his work. Sade discovered, Beauvoir writes, 'that there was
no conciliation possible between his social existence and his private pleasures'. ('Must We Burn Sade?', p.7) Unable to forego his
pleasures he pitted himself against society as it was then constituted, although not against society as such. If the outcome was
an unacceptable ethic, it was society itself that was to blame. To
this extent the ethic is a criticism of society and therein lies
Sade's morality.

Beauvoir arrives at this understanding of Sade on the basis of
an idea borrowed from Hegel's philosophy. At issue, according to
Beauvoir, is the perennial problem of the negotiation of the relationship between the individual and the community: 'can we,
without renouncing our individuality, satisfy our aspirations to
universality?' In his *Phenomenology of Spirit* Hegel presents various
historical-social forms of the concrete realization of this relationship. If the ideal towards which Spirit strives is the overcoming of
the opposition between the individual and the universal (though
these are Beauvoir's, not Hegel's terms), the historical-social
forms it takes along the way are shown to be 'one-sided.' This

means that, historically, one term is realized at the expense of the other. The most famous example of such one-sidedness is the triumph of abstract universality in the aftermath of the French Revolution. In the unmediated negation of the individual 'as a being *existing* in the universal' the death of the individual in the Terror 'has no inner significance or filling . . . It is thus the coldest and meanest of all deaths, with no more significance than cutting off a head of cabbage or swallowing a mouthful of water.'[21]

Within this historical context Sade occupies a complex position. He was, as Beauvoir shows, an apologist for the privilege of the aristocrat, a privilege which he enjoyed and exploited in his first sexual adventures and which he dramatized endlessly in his writings. At the same time, he identified with, not against, the Revolution – famously inciting the rioters from his cell window in the Bastille, citing the murder of the prisoners as their justification. Out of this he becomes, for Beauvoir, emblematic of the protest against the abstract universality represented by the Terror. But what is common to his position throughout, according to Beauvoir, is his championing of the individual – not politically, within a universal system of rights, but metaphysically, as a separate existence. This only becomes comprehensible in the context of a denial of the metaphysically separate subject. In the context of this one-sided denial of the individual, in favour of a presumption of the absolute right of universality, Sade's individual protest, developing into his one-man ethic, however despicable its features, 'assumes a wide human significance'.

Sade's morality consists in his principled protest against the presumption of the absolute right of universality, and his insight into the hypocrisy that maintains it. In a society that respected singularity Sade's 'vices' could have been accepted, recognized as an exception. Instead they are condemned as a threat to the moral and social order. Sade, Beauvoir says, was convinced that 'a man who was content with whipping a prostitute every now and then was less harmful to society than a farmer-general'; that is, less harmful than the burgher who sets himself up as the policeman of decency while profiting from 'the bourgeois hoax which consists in erecting class interests into universal principles.' ('Must We Burn Sade?', p.48) The real plagues, according to Beauvoir, 'are established injustice, official abuses, and constitutional crimes; and these are the inevitable accompaniments of abstract laws which try to impose themselves uniformly upon a plurality of radically separate objects'. ('Must We Burn Sade?', p. 49) In a society so plagued, 'a criminal society', one must become what society calls a criminal as the only way of avoiding complicity with it:

> By means of crime, the libertine refuses any complicity with the evils of the given situation, of which the masses are merely the passive, and hence abject, reflection. It prevents society from reposing in injustice and creates an apocalyptic condition which constrains all individuals to insure their separateness, and thus their truth, in a state of constant tension. ('Must We Burn Sade?', p.58)

The 'supreme value of Sade's testimony' ('Must We Burn Sade?', p.64) is to have forced this truth upon us.

For all this, Beauvoir did not particularly admire Sade – but when it is the historical and social meaning of his work that is at issue admiration is neither here nor there. She did, however, consider his 'solution' to be a failure. For if Sade's desire 'to grasp the very essence of the human condition in terms of his particular situation is the source of his greatness, it is also responsible for his limits'. ('Must We Burn Sade?', p.62) Sade was 'unaware of action' and failed to imagine that there could be any other form of protest than 'individual rebellion'. The possibility of a concrete relation between subjects with a common undertaking – perhaps uniting in the common project of realizing their humanity – did not occur to Sade. This is also the ground of Sade's aesthetic limitations. Lacking any form of detachment from his self he could not 'confront reality and re-create it', but 'contented himself with projecting his fantasies'. ('Must We Burn Sade?', p.37)

Beauvoir's essay on Sade claims our attention today for a number of reasons. It represents Beauvoir at the height of her intellectual powers. In it she condenses the insights of her philosophical work and her mature political understanding into a brilliant and surprising account of the infamous libertine. To this extent it is exemplary of a philosophical interpretation of culture, one that is less concerned with 'being true' to the text than with what we can make of it, for ourselves, in our contemporary context. Beauvoir makes Sade work for her, weaving her interpretation of the old pervert into an implicit criticism of the conservative morality and hypocritical bourgeois universalism of her own time. This is the basis of her identification with him: 'The supreme value of his testimony lies in its ability to disturb us.' ('Must We Burn Sade?', p.64)

10

OLD AGE

The reason that the retired man is rendered hopeless by the want of meaning in his present life is that the meaning of his existence has been stolen from him from the very beginning. A law, as merciless as Lassalle's 'brazen law' of wages, allows him no more than the right to reproduce his life: it refuses him the possibility of discovering any justification for it. When he escapes from the fetters of his trade or calling, all he sees around him is an arid waste: he has not been granted the possibility of committing himself to projects that might have peopled the world with goals, values and reasons for existence.

That is the crime of our society. Its 'old-age policy' is scandalous. But even more scandalous still is the treatment that it inflicts upon the majority of men during their youth and their maturity. It prefabricates the maimed and wretched state that is theirs when they are old. It is the fault of society that the decline of old age begins too early, that it is rapid, physically painful and, because they enter in upon it with empty hands, morally atrocious. Some exploited, alienated individuals inevitably become 'throw-outs', 'rejects', once their strength has failed them.

That is why all the remedies that have been put forward to lessen the distress of the aged are such a mockery: not one of them can possibly repair the systematic destruction that has been inflicted upon some men throughout their lives. Even if they are treated and taken care of, their health cannot be given back. Even if decent houses are built for them, they cannot be provided with the culture, the interests and the responsibilities that would give their life a meaning. I do not say that it would be entirely pointless to improve their condition here and now; but doing so would provide no solution whatsoever to the real problem of old age. What should a society be, so that in his last years a man might still be a man?

Old Age, pp.602–3.

Beauvoir was spurred into writing a book dedicated to the subject of old age by the shocked reaction of readers to what she called the 'hints' at her 'coming old age' at the end of the third volume of her autobiography (1963):

One day I said to myself: 'I'm forty!' By the time I recovered from the shock of that discovery I had reached fifty. The stupor that seized me then has not left me yet . . . To convince myself [of my coming old age], I have but to stand and face my mirror. I thought, one day, when I was forty: 'Deep in that looking glass, old age is watching and waiting for me; and it's inevitable, one day it'll get me.' It's got me now. I often stop, flabbergasted, at the sight of this incredible thing that serves me as a face . . . I loathe my appearance now: the eyebrows slipping down towards the eyes, the bags underneath, the excessive fullness of the cheeks, and that air of sadness around the mouth that wrinkles always bring. (*Force of Circumstance*, p.672)

What is shocking about this passage? It was, Beauvoir decided, the mere fact of speaking about old age, as if it were something obscene. Society looks on old age as a 'shameful secret that it is unseemly to mention': 'What a furious outcry I raised when I offended against this taboo . . . !' (*Old Age*, p.7) What struck Beauvoir as particularly odd in this state of affairs was the glaring

contradiction between the obvious fact of ageing and old age and
the silence in which people tried to shroud it. Looking into the
issue she found that there was no book that dealt with the condition of old people as *The Second Sex* had dealt with the
condition of women, so she set out to write it herself.[22]

Like *The Second Sex*, *Old Age* is divided into two main parts.
The first deals with old age from an external point of view, covering its biological, ethnographical, historical and sociological
aspects. The second deals with it from the point of view of
the lived experience of the ageing and aged, including what
Beauvoir calls its 'existential dimension'. (*Old Age*, p.15) The
book is, overwhelmingly, a depressing read. Beauvoir's research
showed that, while old age may be relatively comfortable for the
wealthy or otherwise lucky few, for the majority it is mostly
hard, miserable, lonely, poverty-stricken and often physically
painful. (Beauvoir took for the starting point of old age the arbitrary figure at which modern industrialized societies usually retire
their workers: 'the old' are those aged sixty-five and over. *Old Age*,
p.19) The treatment of the old demonstrates, Beauvoir says, a contempt for the old that suggests that they are no longer fully human
in the eyes of the young and the middle-aged. This sounds dramatic,
but the weight of the considerable sociological and ethnographical evidence Beauvoir collected bears it out. Accordingly, Beauvoir
saw the various, no doubt well-intentioned and laudable, efforts
to ameliorate the condition of the old as drops in the ocean that
failed to address the 'problem' of old age in any significant or
meaningful way.

Old age is treated – in different ways in Beauvoir's study and
in society generally – as a 'problem'. Of what, exactly, does this
problem consist? For Beauvoir, the biological fact that, biologically, old age brings problems with it – problems of motility,
mental functioning, and so on – is not *the* problem of old age.
Despite these problems, old age is not, *in itself* or necessarily a
problem, though part of the problem of old age is that we treat
it as if it is. For Beauvoir, the refusal to acknowledge ageing and

old age – which is, to a great extent, the refusal to acknowledge death – as an intrinsic part of being human, rather than an unfortunate accident that befalls the human being, is bad faith. It consists of the failure to recognize in the empirical fact of the inevitability of ageing and death an essential part of human existence that is there from the very beginning, rather than a disaster awaiting us in the future, a 'problem to be avoided' if at all possible. One symptom of the bad faith surrounding old age is the lack of serious philosophical literature on it. With *Old Age* Beauvoir thus, once again, tackles a subject that had never before been given such philosophical attention.

For Beauvoir, old age, like everything else, has its existential dimension. The existential analysis of ageing and old age aspires to deal with aspects that transcend the particular, socially and historically located experiences of old age which Beauvoir describes in the first part of the book. It claims to uncover a dimension of *being* old, that is true for all aged human beings, rather than happening to be true for some in certain circumstances. There are two main points. First, old age involves, necessarily, a changed relation to time and therefore, according to Beauvoir, a changed relation with the world and with the individual's own history. (*Old Age*, p.15) This claim is related, but not reducible, to the fact that the old have more past life behind them than they have future life ahead. For Beauvoir – as for any existentialist thinker – human existence is fundamentally temporal. Of course, like everything else – castles, trees, DVDs, and so on – we exist in objective, chronological time. But the relation between time and human existence is more than being in time, it is *being-temporal*. In the philosophical terminology that Beauvoir and Sartre borrowed from Heidegger, we *temporalize* time, which means that human existence *produces* time for itself as an active differentiation between past, present, and future. In the simplest terms, there *is only* time *for* human existence and the meaning of human existence can only be understood on the basis of this relation to time. This does not mean that chronological time – measured in years, minutes,

and so on, according to cosmological or microphysical regulari-
ties – is not the same for each of us, or that we cannot locate ourselves in it. But the temporalization of time by human existence is
basic to the measurement of objective, chronological time and
gives it its meaning.

For Beauvoir, as for all existentialists, the being-temporal of
human existence involves a certain priority of the future. To
exist is to continually surpass what one was or is in projecting
towards the future, such that the meaning of the individual's
present and past is forever changing in relation to their future-
directed projects. This is why therapies like psychoanalysis do not
necessarily uncover the final 'truth' of one's past, but, rather, give
that past a truth in relation to the future. If we are continually
reinterpreting our own past this is not because we fail to grasp
the one, true interpretation, but because the meaning of the
past is, fundamentally, changing.

What difference does it make, then, when, in old age, we face
'a limited future and a frozen past' (*Old Age*, p.421)? According
to Beauvoir, whereas the young easily surpass the past in bound-
ing towards the future, the weight of the past slows the old
down, even bringing the old person to a halt. (*Old Age*, p.435)
We see in the old, Beauvoir says, a tendency to turn towards the
past. If, for each of us, the time which we look upon as our own
is that at which we conceive and carry out our projects (*Old Age*,
p.484), the old feel that the time that 'belongs' to them, in which
their projects were conceived and executed, was a former time.
This explains, Beauvoir says, the curious phrase 'in my time'. In
its most extreme formulation: 'Apart from some exceptions, the
old man no longer *does* anything. He is defined by an *exis*, not by
a *praxis*: a being, not a doing.' (*Old Age*, p.244) The uncomfortable conclusion of Beauvoir's argument is that old age is
existentially, and not just biologically, a radically transformed
state of being. If human existence *is* the surpassing or transcend-
ing of the past in the projection towards the future, then, in
some sense, the old no longer *are* human.

The second main point in Beauvoir's existential analysis of old age initially seems to sit uneasily with the first. Beauvoir claims that the 'discovery' of old age is, for each of us, imposed from the outside, rather than experienced from within. Furthermore, there is no 'full inward experience' of old age (*Old Age*, p.324), which means that, existentially, our being-old is a condition somewhat at odds with our subjective existence. In explaining this Beauvoir makes use of the distinction – borrowed from Hegel – between two different modes of human existence, our 'being-for-ourselves' and our 'being-for-others'. (Traditionally, these phrases are hyphenated to emphasize that they refer to an existential structure, rather than an empirical state of affairs.) Although we are 'for-ourselves' the subject of our actions and the absolute free origin of our projects, we are 'for-others' the object of various actions: curiosity, concern, pity, love, contempt and so on. (This was what Beauvoir earlier described as one dimension of the 'tragic ambiguity' of human existence.) The meaning of the word 'object' here is double. On the one hand we are 'object' in the grammatical sense, with no pejorative implication. On the other, we are 'object' in the sense that we are reduced to an object and denied recognition as a subject. In both cases, though, what we *are*, in the eyes of the other, is necessarily not what we *are* for ourselves. According to Beauvoir, I can only be an object for myself through the eyes of the other: in order to see what figure I cut I must see myself as others see me. Even so, the discrepancy between my being-for-myself and my being-for-others can never be overcome.

The analysis of the relationship between being-for-self and being-for-the-other holds quite generally, for any aspect of our public existence. I discover that I am beautiful or ugly, brave or cowardly, 'good' or 'evil', in the context of my relations with others, *through* the others. As a general problem it is one of the most insistent themes of Beauvoir's early fiction, especially *The Blood of Others*. The peculiarity of the situation of being old is that what we discover is that we have changed. Precisely because we were once young, we discover, with surprise, that 'suddenly' we are old: 'When I was fifty I gave a start when an American student told me that one of his friends had said, "So, Simone de Beauvoir is an old woman, then!"' (*Old Age*, p.320) It is precisely because old age is thus conferred on us from outside that we can be old when we are biologically relatively young, and young even in advanced years. (*Old Age*, p.325) It also reveals the fundamental mistake – the pathetic delusion – in the claim that 'you are only as old as you feel'. You are, on the contrary, as old as the others say you are.

In certain situations, the relationship between our being-for-self and our being-for-others becomes a psycho-social and political, as well as existential problem, or the existential problem is dramatically intensified. In *Black Skin, White Masks* (1952) Frantz Fanon described his situation – a black man from the French colonies studying in Paris in the late 1930s – as one in which he was 'overdetermined from without'. 'Fixed' by the white eyes upon him, he became aware of what he was for those others when he entered a room: 'not a new man who has come in but a new kind of man, a new genus. Why, it's a nigger!'[23] Nothing but a nigger. A psychoanalytic psychotherapist by profession, Fanon used the existentialist distinction between being-for-self and being-for-others to explain the psychopathology of colonized black people. He found that many of them were psychically deformed by the interiorization of racist images of themselves.

Old age does not, perhaps, represent a psychic disfigurement of this order, although the degraded and abused old people in our hospitals ('bed blockers') and 'old folks'' homes, or those living at home on their pittance pensions, might disagree. For Beauvoir the problem of old age arises because the old are *reduced to* their old age, becoming nothing but 'an old person', or any of the number of pejorative names for the old that our languages boast. For Beauvoir the old are, in the eyes of the young, 'a "different species", one in whom they do not recognize themselves . . .

the aged person is no more than a corpse under suspended sentence'. (*Old Age*, p.244) Echoing her analysis of racism in the USA, Beauvoir contends that the contradiction between the shameful treatment of the old and 'the humanist morality' on which our societies are allegedly based can only be understood by presuming that we have silently adopted the 'convenient plan' of refusing to consider the old as 'real people'. (*Old Age*, p.8) This, in turn, is made possible by the bad faith of the young, who refuse to see their own fate in the condition of the old. This is why the discovery of one's old age is an unpleasant shock. One becomes a problem, a burden, a useless, unproductive drain on society's resources: 'do not resuscitate'. In old age what is conferred on us from outside – and what is so hard to accept – is the image of a redundant, feeble-minded, half-human.

In Beauvoir's account the two existential aspects of old age – the changing relation to time and the discovery of old age in one's being-for-others – are described in unremittingly negative terms. If we read her as claiming that she is describing something inevitable, *Old Age* would be a reactionary and unpleasant, as well as empirically contestable, book. But this is not what she is claiming. As well as frequently acknowledging cultural and historical variants and individual exceptions, the emphasis of the analysis is, throughout, on a broadly historical and socio-economic account of the way in which the existential aspects are experienced. To this extent the form of the analysis in *Old Age* is the culmination of over forty years of Beauvoir's work. In the last two volumes of her autobiography (1963, 1972) Beauvoir identified the main problem with *The Second Sex* as the 'idealistic and a priori struggle of consciousnesses'. (*Force of Circumstance*, p.202) 'Today,' she wrote in the last volume, 'I should provide a materialistic, not an idealistic, theoretical foundation for the opposition between the Same and the Other. I should base the rejection and oppression of the Other not on antagonistic awareness but upon the economic explanation of scarcity.' (*All Said and Done*, pp.483–4) In *Old Age* this 'materialism' wins out. In every move, the socio-economic explanation trumps every other in importance. Beauvoir's description of the experience of the existential aspects of old age is not proposed as inevitable. It describes how old age is lived, by all but the privileged few, under current conditions, and it does so precisely in order that current conditions should cease to prevail.

If the old man 'no longer *does* anything', existing in the present only to dwell on the past, this is because he was not 'granted the possibility of committing himself to projects that might have peopled the world with goals, values and reasons for existence'. In being condemned to a life of subsistence labour his future was 'stolen from him from the very beginning'. Deprived of a youth and middle age of free, creative labour we cannot be provided in old age 'with the culture, the interests and the responsibilities' that would give our lives meaning. The revelation of old age as the forced assumption of the degraded image of society's flotsam is not our inevitable fate, but the consequence of society's unwillingness to face what it has made of old age and, more importantly, what would be necessary to change this:

> for it is the exploitation of the workers, the pulverization of society, and the utter poverty of a culture confined to the privileged, educated few that leads to this kind of dehumanized old age. And it is this old age that makes it clear that everything has to be reconsidered, recast from the very beginning. That is why the whole problem is so carefully passed over in silence: and that is why this silence has to be shattered. (*Old Age*, p.13–4)

The implication of *Old Age* is that the analysis of the existential aspects of old age – and indeed of everything else – must itself be seen as historically located. In relation to Beauvoir's previous work, this is the most radical move in the book as it brings into question the alleged universality of the existential analyses of many of her earlier books. But what makes *Old Age* Beauvoir's most radical work is her 'revolutionary' conclusion that 'old age

is a problem on which all the failures of a society converge'.[24]
What should a society be, so that in our last years we might still
be human? Beauvoir offers no blueprint, but lays down a challenge, characteristic of her work as a whole, that, in our ageing,
pension crisis-ridden societies, we cannot afford to ignore: 'It is
the whole system that is at issue and our claim cannot be otherwise than radical – change life itself.' (*Old Age*, p.604)

NOTES

1: Deirdre Bair, *Simone de Beauvoir: A Biography*, Summit Books, New York, 1990, p.432.

2: G. W. F. Hegel, *Phenomenology of Spirit*, trans. A. V. Miller, Oxford University Press, Oxford, 1977, pp.49, 50.

3: 'Ontology' is traditionally the name given to the enquiry into the nature and meaning of 'being'. Ontological claims are claims about different kinds of things at the level of their being.

4: 'Existentialism and Humanism', trans. Philip Mairet, in Jean-Paul Sartre, *Basic Writings*, edited by Stephen Priest, Routledge, London and New York, 2001.

5: The references to contemporary events in this extract are explained in Kristana Arp's footnotes to her translation of 'An Eye for an Eye'. At Kharkov, in the Ukraine, a war crimes tribunal condemned four to death. Joseph Darnand was the head of the French collaborationist militia. Paul Ferdonnet and Jean Hérold Pacquis were both Nazi propagandist radio broadcasters. All three were executed. 642 people were killed at Oradour sur Glane (in Limousin) when German soldiers locked them in the church and set fire to it.

6: Orlando Patterson, *Slavery and Social Death*, Harvard University Press, Cambridge Mass., 1982.

7: In this part of her trip Beauvoir is accompanied by 'N'; her friend Natalie Sorokine Moffatt.

8: Unfortunately H. M. Parshley's 1953 English translation of *The Second Sex* is seriously deficient. It is an abridged version of Beauvoir's original (cutting around 15 per cent of the text) which systematically mistranslates the philosophical terminology, often translating Beauvoir's points into their exact opposite. However, the publisher who holds the translation rights (Knopf) does not allow retranslations. I have therefore been forced to use extracts from Parshley's translation, choosing so as to avoid the very worst of the problems.

9: Bair, *Simone de Beauvoir*, p.617.

10: This is the title of the fifth chapter of Fanon's *Black Skin, White Masks*, trans. Charles Lam Markmann, Pluto Press, London, 1986. Unfortunately Markmann's translation makes many of the same errors with the existentialist vocabulary as Parshley's translation of *The Second Sex*.

11: This point has been developed in detail by Sonia Kruks, 'Beauvoir: The Weight of Situation', in Elizabeth Fallaize, ed., *Simone de Beauvoir: A Critical Reader*, Routledge, London and New York, 1998.

12: Anxious to escape the philosophical baggage weighing down our use of traditional terms, Heidegger avoided the German equivalents of the English 'human', referring to that entity which we ourselves are as *Dasein* (a common German word which would normally be translated as 'existence'). In common with most of her contemporaries, and with none of Heidegger's linguistic scruples, Beauvoir translated '*Dasein*' into French as '*l'existence humaine*' or '*la réalité humanine*' – 'human existence' or 'human reality'.

13: The masculinity studies of the 1990s recognized the need to rethink what it meant to be a man, but its analyses were mainly psychological and sociological. The existential-ontological question – what is a man? – has yet to receive any sustained investigation.

14: Now available online: http://www.womynkind.org/scum.htm

15: See Stella Sandford, 'Contingent Ontologies: Sex, Gender and "Woman" in Simone de Beauvoir and Judith Butler', *Radical Philosophy* 97, September/October 1999.

16: This example comes from Anne Fausto-Sterling, *Sexing the Body*, Basic Books, New York, 2000, pp.116–27.

17: Ibid., p.51.

18: Jean-Paul Sartre, *The Transcendence of the Ego*, trans. Forrest Williams and Robert Kirkpatrick, Hill and Wang, New York, 1960, pp.40, 41, 63.

19: In modern European philosophy there is an important distinction between the 'transcendental ego' and the 'transcendent ego'. However, the two words 'transcendent' and 'transcendental' are sometimes (confusingly) used synonymously, and here Beauvoir's 'transcendental' is synonymous with Sartre's 'transcendent'.

20: Alice Schwartzer, *Simone de Beauvoir aujourd 'hui: six entretiens*, traduits de l'allemand par Léa Marcou, Mercure de France, Paris, 1984.

21: Hegel, *Phenomenology of Spirit*, p.360.

22: Beauvoir made these comments in an interview with Nina Sutton in *The Guardian*, 16th February 1970. See Bair, *Simone de Beauvoir*, pp.539–40.

23: Fanon, *Black Skin, White Masks*, p.116.

24: Interview with Sutton, in Bair, *Simone de Beauvoir*, p.540.

CHRONOLOGY

1908 9 January, Simone-Ernestine-Lucie-Marie Bertrand de Beauvoir born to Françoise (née Brasseur) and George de Beauvoir, Paris.

1910 9 June, Hélène de Beauvoir, sister to Simone, born, Paris.

1913–25 Educated at Institut Adeline Désire, Paris (Baccalaureat awarded 1924–5).

1927–8 Studied for degree in literature, Latin, Greek and philosophy at Institut Sante-Marie, Neuilly.

1928–9 Studied philosophy at the Sorbonne and Ecole Normale Supérieure. First meeting with Jean-Paul Sartre; lifelong relationship begins.

1929 Awarded Agrégée de Philosophie.

1931–3 Held teaching position at Lycée Montgrand, Marseille.

1933–7 Held teaching position at Lycée Jeanne d'Arc, Rouen.

1938–43 Held teaching position at Molière (Passy) and Lycée Camille-Sée, Paris.

1939 Beginning of mobilization in France; Sartre drafted to Nancy.

1940 Sartre captured and imprisoned as POW.

1941 Sartre released. Failed attempts to enter Resistance.

1943 Beauvoir's first novel, *She Came to Stay* (*L'invitée*), published.

1944 *Pyrrhus and Cineas* published.

1945 Co-founded *Les temps modernes*. Beauvoir's first play, *Who Shall Die?* (*Les bouches inutiles*), published. *The Blood of Others* (*Le sang des autres*) published.

1946 'An Eye for An Eye' (*L'oeil pour oeil*), 'Literature and Metaphysics' ('Littérature et métaphysique') and *All Men are Mortal* published.

1947 First trip to the USA. First meeting with Nelson Algren. *The Ethics of Ambiguity* (*Pour une morale de l'ambiguïté*) published.

1948 *America Day by Day* (*L'Amérique au jour le jour*) published.

1949 *The Second Sex* (*Le deuxième sexe*) published.

1951 'Must We Burn Sade?' ('Faut-il brûler Sade?') published.

1954 *The Mandarins* (*Les Mandarins*) published.

1958 First volume of autobiography, *Memoirs of a Dutiful Daughter* (*Mémoires d'une jeune fille rangée*) published.

1960 Second volume of autobiography, *The Prime of Life* (*La force de l'âge*) published.

1963 Third volume of autobiography, *Force of Circumstance* (*La forces des choses*), published.

1964 *A Very Easy Death* (*Une morte très douce*) published.

1967 First collection of short stories, *The Woman Destroyed* (*La femme rompue*), published.

1970 *Old Age* (*La vieillesse*) published.

1971 Beauvoir added her signature to the 'Manifesto of 343', declaring that she had had an abortion, still illegal in France.

1972 Fourth and final volume of autobiography, *All Said and Done* (*Tout compte fait*) published.

1980 Death of Sartre.

1981 *Adieux: A Farewell to Sartre* (*Le cérémonie des adieux*) published. Death of Algren.

1986 14 April, death of Beauvoir, Paris.

1990 *Letters to Sartre* (*Lettres à Sartre*) published, edited by Beauvoir's adopted daughter Sylvie le Bon de Beauvoir.

1997 *Beloved Chicago Man: Letters to Nelson Algren 1947–1964* (*Lettres à Nelson Algren: un amour transatlantique: 1947–64*), published, edited by Sylvie le Bon de Beauvoir.

PRIMARY SOURCES

Adieux: A Farewell to Sartre, trans. Patrick O'Brian, Penguin, London, 1985. *Le Cérémonie des adieux*.

All Said and Done (Autobiography, Volume 4), trans. Patrick O'Brian, Penguin, London, 1977.

America Day by Day, trans. Carol Cosman, Victor Gollancz, London, 1998.

A Very Easy Death, trans. Patrick O' Brian, Penguin, London, 1969.

Beloved Chicago Man: Letters to Nelson Algren 1947–64, Phoenix, London, 1999.

The Blood of Others, trans. Yvonne Moyse and Roger Senhouse, Penguin, London, 1964. *Le sang des autres*.

The Ethics of Ambiguity, trans. Bernard Frechtman, Citadel, New York, 1976.

'An Eye for An Eye', trans. Kristana Arp, in Margaret A. Simons et al., eds, *Simone de Beauvoir: Philosophical Writings*, University of Illinois Press, Urbana and Chicago, 2004.

Force of Circumstance (Autobiography, Volume 3), trans. Richard Howard, Penguin, London, 1968.

'Literature and Metaphysics', trans. Véronique Zaytzeff and Frederick M. Morrison, in Margaret A. Simons et al., eds, *Simone de Beauvoir: Philosophical Writings*, University of Illinois Press, Urbana and Chicago, 2004.

The Mandarins, trans. Leonard M. Friedman, Collins, London, 1957. *Les mandarins*, Gallimard, Paris, 1954.

Memoirs of a Dutiful Daughter (Autobiography, Volume 1), trans. James Kirkup, Penguin, London, 1963.

'Must We Burn Sade?', trans. Annette Michelson (revised by Austryn Wainhouse and Richard Seaver) in Marquis de Sade, *The 120 Days of Sodom and Other Writings*, Austryn Wainhouse and Richard Seaver, eds, Grove Press, New York, 1966.

Old Age, trans. Patrick O' Brian, Penguin, London, 1977.

The Prime of Life (Autobiography, Volume 2), trans. Peter Green, Penguin, London, 1965.

Pyrrhus and Cineas, trans. Marybeth Timmerman, in Margaret A. Simons et al., eds, *Simone de Beauvoir: Philosophical Writings*, University of Illinois Press, Urbana and Chicago, 2004.

She Came to Stay, trans. Yvonne Moyse and Roger Senhouse, Fontana, London, 1984. *L'invitée*.

The Second Sex, trans. H. M. Parshley, Picador, London, 1988.

The Woman Destroyed, trans. Patrick O'Brian, Flamingo, London, 1984. *La femme rompue*.

SUGGESTIONS FOR FURTHER READING

Books by Beauvoir

Apart from the major texts discussed in this book, the following titles are a great way to begin reading Beauvoir. Unfortunately, many of Beauvoir's works are now out of print (both in French and in English translation), though it may be hoped that on the occasion of the centenary of her birth, in 2008, new editions of some may appear. All four volumes of Beauvoir's autobiography, but especially the second (*The Prime of Life*, covering the occupation and liberation of Paris and Beauvoir's early years with Sartre) offer a fascinating and enjoyable introduction to Beauvoir's life and times. *Beloved Chicago Man: Letters to Nelson Algren 1947–64*, written in English, is intimate but also funny and informative. *A Very Easy Death* is a frank reflection on the death of Beauvoir's mother and *Adieux: A Farewell to Sartre* (*Le Cérémonie des adieux*) a sometimes brutal account of Sartre's last days, together with transcripts of late, staged conversations between Beauvoir and Sartre. Beauvoir's first two novels, *She Came to Stay* (*L'invitée*), and *The Blood of Others* (*Le sang des autres*), are good examples of Beauvoir's metaphysical fiction. There is general agreement, however, that *The Mandarins* (*Les mandarins*) is Beauvoir's best novel (it was awarded the prestigious Prix Goncourt in the year of its publication). The collection of short stories, *The Woman Destroyed* (*La femme rompue*) is exemplary of the relationship between existentialist philosophy, feminism and literature in Beauvoir's mature work.

Books on Beauvoir

The best general biography of Beauvoir is Deirdre Bair's *Simone de Beauvoir: A Biography* (Summit, New York, 1990). Toril Moi's *Simone de Beauvoir: The Making of An Intellectual Woman* (Blackwell, Oxford, 1994) is a more academic, but nonetheless accessible, intellectual biography with some detailed examination of selected texts. Good examples of recent critical and philosophical work on Beauvoir, from Europe and the United States, can be found in Emily R. Grosholz ed., *The Legacy of Simone de Beauvoir*, Clarendon Press, Oxford, 2004. In the last decade a handful of good books on Beauvoir's contribution to philosophy have also been published in English or English translation. These include Kristana Arp, *The Bonds of Freedom: Simone de Beauvoir's Existentialist Ethics*, Open Court, Illinois, 2001; Nancy Bauer, *Simone de Beauvoir, Philosophy and Feminism*, Columbia University Press, New York, 2001; Eleanore Holveck, *Simone de Beauvoir's Philosophy of Lived Experience: Literature and Metaphysics*, Rowman & Littlefield, Lanham, 2002; Karen Vintges, *Philosophy as Passion: The Thinking of Simone de Beauvoir*, trans. Anne Lavelle, Indiana University Press, Bloomington and Indianapolis, 1996.

INDEX

Beauvoir is indicated by 'B'.